LBERT CAMUS

MODERN MASTERS

EDITED BY frank kermode

albert camus

OF EUROPE AND AFRICA

conor cruise o'brien

NEW YORK | THE VIKING PRESS

ACKNOWLEDGMENTS

Alfred A. Knopf, Inc.: From *The Plague* by Albert
Camus, Copyright 1948 by Stuart Gilbert; from *The
Stranger* by Albert Camus, Copyright 1946 by Alfred
A. Knopf, Inc.; from *The Fall* by Albert Camus,
Copyright © 1956 by Alfred A. Knopf, Inc.

The Macmillan Company: From "The Great Day"
from *Collected Poems* by William Butler Yeats,
Copyright 1940 by Georgie Yeats, renewed 1968 by
Bertha Georgie Yeats, Michael Butler Yeats, and
Anne Yeats, reprinted with permission of The Mac-
millan Company and A. P. Watt and Son, Ltd.

CONTENTS

ALBERT CAMUS

The Stranger

i

Albert Camus was born on November 7, 1913, in the village of Mondovi near Constantine in Algeria. His father, Lucien Camus, a cellarman in the wine trade, was of Alsatian origin. He died of wounds received at the Battle of the Marne in the year after Camus's birth. Camus's mother, Catherine Sintès, who was of Spanish origin, had never learned to read or write and, as a widow, earned a living for her family as a charwoman. Camus, his elder brother Lucien, his mother, his grandmother, and a paralyzed uncle shared a two-room apartment in the working-class district of Belcourt.

A child coming from such a home would in many societies have had little chance of getting a first-class or even a good education. The French educational system has, however, tried to make good—at least for children of European culture—the French Revolution's principle of equality of opportunity: *la carrière ouverte aux talents.* In primary school Camus attracted the attention of his teacher, Louis Germain, who prepared him for a scholarship in the Lycée in Algiers. At the age of thirteen he was already reading Gide, Montherlant, and Malraux, and Malraux in particular was to have a strong influence on him. Football and swimming were his principal passions at this time, and swimming retains an almost sacramental significance in his work. In 1930 he had his first attack of tuberculosis and had to leave his overcrowded home. He stayed for a time with an uncle, Acault, a butcher with literary interests, described as of "Voltairean and anarchist tradition." In 1932, at the University of Algiers, Camus fell under the influence of Jean Grenier, to whom he dedicated two of his early books and who, as he said, gave him a taste for philosophical speculation.

His first political commitment seems to date from 1933, when he joined the anti-fascist Amsterdam-Pleyel movement founded by Henri Barbusse and Romain Rolland. His first marriage took place in 1934 and broke up a little more than a year after. At the end of 1934 Camus joined the Communist Party and is said to have served it as a propaganda agent among the Arabs. He was later to say that he had left the party in 1935 at a time when the party line—of Franco-Russian friendship in the Popular Front period—required a playing down of colonial injustices and therefore a reduced interest in, among others, the Arabs of Algeria. It does not seem, however, that Camus can have broken with the party in any distinct way at this date since the following year finds him at the head of the Maison de Culture in Algiers, which was under the control of the Communist Party. It seems more probable that he broke with the party in 1937.[1]

While pursuing his studies in philosophy at the University of Algiers, Camus worked irregularly as a spare-parts salesman and in various clerical jobs. From 1935 on, he wrote the essays which were later to be published as *L'Envers et l'Endroit* (*Betwixt and Between*). He also founded the Théâtre du Travail, for which in 1936 he wrote his first play, *Révolte dans les Asturies*. In 1936 and 1937 he was working as an actor in the touring company sponsored by Radio Algiers, and in 1937 he became a journalist on *Alger Républicain*. For health reasons it was impossible for him to present himself for the Agrégation examination, which is the normal culmination for the type of education he had received and which would have opened a career for him in the state service. In 1938 he wrote his second play, *Caligula*, and began prelim-

---

[1] Not only the date but the circumstances of Camus's break with the party remain obscure, like much else in his early life. See the section "*Politique et Culture Mediterranéennes*," reprinted in R. Quilliot (ed.), *Albert Camus: Essais* (Paris, 1965). Anne Durand, in *Le Cas Albert Camus* (Paris, 1961), suggests that his real reason for leaving the party was that its policies tended to "the abandonment of populations which were undoubtedly 'French,' in heart if not in race."

inary work on an essay on the Absurd, which he was later to publish as *Le Mythe de Sisyphe*, and also on the notes for his first novel, *L'Etranger*. In 1939 his book of essays *Noces*—on which he had begun work in 1937—was published, and he carried out for his paper an inquiry into destitution in the Kabyle region of Algeria. On the outbreak of the war he volunteered for military service but was rejected on health grounds. In 1940 occurred his second marriage, with Francine Faure, a girl from Oran, and in this year also, as a result of conflicts with censorship, Camus's paper collapsed and he left Algeria for Paris. In May he finished *L'Etranger*, and in the same month he had to leave Paris with the staff of *Paris Soir* (for which he was then working), as a result of the German invasion. In January 1941 he returned to Oran, where he taught in a private school. There in February he finished *Le Mythe de Sisyphe* (*The Myth of Sisyphus*).

In 1941, at the age of twenty-eight, Camus had completed three of the works for which he is principally remembered today: the play *Caligula*, the novel *L'Etranger*, and the long philosophical essay *Le Mythe de Sisyphe*. These works are quite closely connected, and it is convenient to regard them as forming the first of three main phases of his work: the phase of the Stranger.

Before discussing these works, it is necessary to say something, to ask some questions, and to register the existence of some blank areas, regarding the social and political context in which these remarkable works were shaped.

The Algeria in which Camus grew up was in theory not a colony but an integral part of the French Republic, consisting of three overseas departments. The realities of its history and life belonged, however, to the colonial experience. It had been annexed by France in 1836: Camus's father's people had settled there in 1871. The inhabitants of the country consisted of a minority of mixed European origin, for whom the idea of forming part of France had a certain reality, and a majority of Arab and Berber origin, speaking Arabic and professing the Moslem religion. For them, forming part of the French Republic was not a reality, although it was for some of them, for a time, an aspiration.

What was the relation of Camus, growing up among the poorest of the European working class, to the Moslem and Arabic-speaking people who made up the bulk of the population of the city in which he lived?

Commentators on Camus have not on the whole paid much attention to this question. Yet it may, I suggest, be of importance for his work and in particular for his treatment of the themes of the Stranger and the Absurd.

For Madame Germaine Brée, who probably has done more than anyone else to shape the ideas about Camus prevalent among English-speaking people, there is no problem here. She tells us that Camus described "as none before him" not only the beauty of the African coast and the glory of an inexhaustible sun, but "also the peculiar temperament, ethics, attitudes and language of the native Algerians, with whom he felt more at home than with anyone else." She goes on: "Of French, Spanish, Italian, Maltese and Jewish extraction—European, Berber and Arabic—the working-class population of Belcourt is impervious to the racial barriers that exist in more prosperous middle-class milieux. The Berber and Arab never seemed 'strangers' to Camus."[2]

A working-class population "impervious to racial barriers" would be an unusual phenomenon. A population which could attain this condition when the barriers were not only "of race" but also of religion, language, and culture, all reinforcing "race"—as in the case of the dividing line between European and Arab in Algeria—would be unique. And Camus's writings do not in fact reflect any such state of affairs, as we shall see.

During the last six years of Camus's life, Algeria was torn by bitter fighting which divided Europeans from native Moslems, and working-class Europeans were among the most determined supporters of the French army and most bitter enemies of the Moslem *fellagha*. No such open struggle was, of course, going on in Camus's youth, but neither is there any serious reason to suppose that the idyllic interracial conditions described by Mme. Brée existed during this period.[3]

---

[2] Germaine Brée, *Camus* (rev. ed., New York, 1964).
[3] In the first chapter of *Camus* (1964 ed.), Mme. Brée inexplicably states that Camus's 1958 position on the

From Camus himself we learn little, directly, about what the relation actually was. His efforts as a propagandist among the Moslems seem to have left as little trace on his work as they did on the Moslems. Indeed his collected works as we have them today show almost no trace of any living relation either to Communists or to Arabs. His intellectual culture is that of the French middle-class youth of his time: Nietzsche, Barrès, and Gide are powerful influences. There is little or no trace of Marxist influence on his thought, other than what may have been—rather doubtfully—transmitted through Malraux. The poverty of his childhood—reflected most distinctly in the early essays, *L'Envers et l'Endroit*—has marked him for life: in his health, in "an instinctive horror, never overcome, of banisters," and no doubt in the quality of his loneliness, despair, and joy. But there is also a sense in which poverty and distance make French middle-class culture more attractive to him than they are to born members of the French middle class. Thus, where Jean-Paul Sartre, born into that class, rejects its good manners, elegance, and sense of literary tradition and writes a surly, conversational, ungraceful French, Camus writes with a spare and conscious elegance, evoking, as did

Algerian war—which we will consider in due course— "seems now to have prevailed among Algerians whether of European or of Arabic extraction." As Camus's position by 1958 was that the French army should remain in Algeria to protect the Europeans, the continued assertion of the view that it "prevailed among Algerians . . . of Arabic extraction" in 1964, after the withdrawal both of the army and of most of the Europeans, seems a little comic. In 1959, when the statement was first written, it was just wrong.

Gide, the memory of the seventeenth and eighteenth centuries. He has been criticized for putting too refined and metropolitan a French into the mouths of his Algerian characters.[4]

The French educational system was, as is well known, identical in all parts of France, including Algeria: it is also an exceptionally thorough and strenuous system. European and part French by birth, Camus became thoroughly French by education. This rather obvious fact has been to some extent disguised, not only by some of the commentaries on him, but also by some of his own writings. In a lecture delivered at the Maison de la Culture in February 1937, he spoke of rehabilitating a Mediterranean culture: "North Africa is one of the few countries where East and West live together, and at this confluence there is no difference between the manner of life of a Spaniard or an Italian of the quays of Algiers and the Arabs who are around him. The most essential element in the Mediterranean genius springs perhaps from this encounter, unique in history and geography, born between East and West. . . . This truth of a Mediterranean culture exists and manifests itself on every point: one, linguistic unity, facility of learning one Latin language when one knows another; two, unity of origin, prodigious

---

[4] Anne Durand, a French-Algerian contemporary of Camus's, writes as follows about the opening words of *L'Etranger*: "But we Algerians are pulled up by the first words: 'Today mother [*maman*] died . . .' Among us *Maman* is used as a vocative, never otherwise. *Never*, you know it well." She goes on to speak of Meursault as an "*espèce de gentleman*. . . . The Meursault in question is a stranger to us."

collectivism of the Middle Ages, order of knights, order of religious feudalities, et cetera."[5]

The interest of these words—in an early and ephemeral statement—lies in their contradictions. At the very moment when he wishes to affirm the unity of the Mediterranean world, the marriage of East and West, he reveals himself as incapable of thinking in any categories other than those of a Frenchman. Although he rejects Maurras's conception of "the Latin West" with its pro-fascist associations—at this time of Mussolini's invasion of Ethiopia—his own Mediterranean truth reposes on a supposed linguistic unity derived from the similarity of the Romance languages: and this in a country of which the majority of the inhabitants were Arabic-speaking. The terms in which he defines the supposed "unity of origin" of this culture all seem to be European and related to the Crusades. Although in the course of this paper Camus refers to many European names and achievements he has nothing to say of any other contribution to the culture of the area except for a single vague reference to "the great Oriental thoughts." It is quite clear, though never explicitly stated, that his Mediterranean culture is a European one and in Algeria a French one, and that the Arabs who have a part in this culture will have become French Arabs.

For Frantz Fanon, writing years later out of his experience in the Algerian war, the vital distinction was between *le colon* (the settler) and *le colonisé*.

[5] "*La Culture Indigène: La Nouvelle Culture Mediterranéenne*," reprinted in Quilliot, op. cit., pp. 1321–27.

There could be no cultural unity between them, and the relation between them was one of implicit or explicit violence. Fanon's picture is itself a violent and Manichean one and his book, *The Wretched of the Earth*, was an act of war, in time of war. One need not accept it fully and literally, but one can see well enough, at least in retrospect, that it had enough truth in it, in Algeria as in other colonial situations, for a point of view which ignored even the possibility of its existence to be unrealistic to the point of fantasy. A gentler, subtler, and more divided writer than Fanon, the Tunisian Jew Albert Memmi, in his book *The Colonizer and the Colonized* has a chapter about the left-wing colonizer, "the colonizer who refuses." Much of what Memmi has to say applies to Camus's position as it developed in the postwar period, rather than to the period with which we are now concerned, a time when the possibility of Algeria's ceasing to be "French" had occurred to few. But Memmi's central point—that left-wing intellectuals, even Communists, unconspicuously shared the assumptions of a colonialism which they consciously rejected—remains relevant. Camus was (it seems) still a Communist at the time when he evolved a conception of "Mediterranean culture" which in fact served to legitimize France's possession of Algeria.

The point here is not that Camus was acting in a wicked or hypocritical way. On the contrary, as his articles in *Misère en Kabylie* and elsewhere show, he was honorably insistent that France in Algeria should live up to her professions, and this insistence more than once got him into trouble. The point is rather that in the position of the left-wing colonist there are usually strong elements of estrangement, unreality, and even hallucination: when a brilliantly intelligent and well-educated man, who has lived all his life surrounded by an Arabic-speaking population, affirms the existence of a form of unity including the Arabs and based on the Romance languages, it is not excessive to speak of hallucination. It is important for the better understanding both of Camus's work and of his political development—and the two are intertwined—to try to grasp this situation from the outset. Camus is a stranger on the African shore, and surrounded by people who are strangers in that France of which they are legally supposed to be a part. The splendidly rationalist system of education which molded Camus was propagating, in relation to his own social context, a myth: that of French Algeria.

With this in mind, let us consider Camus's first novel, *L'Etranger* (*The Stranger*).

The hero or anti-hero of *L'Etranger* is called Meursault. He has a job as a clerk in Algiers. "Mersault" was a pen name which Camus had used in journalism, and he himself had worked as a clerk during a part of his student life.

The novel opens with the words: "Mother died today or, maybe, yesterday; I can't be sure."[6] The opening pages describe, with great precision of physical detail, Meursault's journey to the Home where his

---

[6] See note 4, above.

mother died, and the funeral. The narrator's feelings are not directly indicated, but various blanks and silences show that his feelings are not quite those expected of him: "The Warden went on talking but I didn't pay much attention. Finally he said: 'Now I suppose you'd like to see your mother?' I rose without replying, and he led the way to the door."

He surprises the mortuary-keeper by declining to look at his mother's body. On the day of the funeral: "A morning breeze was blowing and it had a pleasant salty tang. There was the promise of a very fine day. I hadn't been in the country for ages, and I caught myself thinking what an agreeable walk I could have had, if it hadn't been for Mother." Later on, during the funeral itself: "Now, in the full glare of the morning sun, with everything shimmering in the heat haze, there was something inhuman, discouraging, about this landscape."

On the following day, a Saturday, back in Algiers, he goes swimming and meets a girl, Marie Cardona, whom he has known slightly before. "When we had dressed, she stared at my black tie and asked if I was in mourning. I explained that my mother had died. 'When?' she asked, and I said 'Yesterday.' She made no remark, though I thought she shrank away a little."

They go to a Fernandel movie together, and Marie goes back with Meursault to his flat. "When I woke up, Marie had gone. She'd told me her aunt expected her first thing in the morning. I remembered it was a Sunday, and that put me off; I've never cared for Sundays. So I turned my head and lazily sniffed the smell of brine that Marie's head had left on the pillow." Meursault spends Sunday in his room, watching the people in the street below.

The following evening, after a routine day at the office, Meursault meets an elderly neighbor, Salamano, who has a dog which he is in the habit of beating: "You can see them in the rue de Lyon, the dog pulling his master along as hard as he can, till finally the old chap misses a step and nearly falls. Then he beats his dog and calls it names. The dog cowers and lags behind, and it's his master's turn to drag him along. Presently the dog forgets, starts tugging at the leash again, gets another hiding and more abuse. Then they halt on the pavement, the pair of them, and glare at each other; the dog with terror and the man with hatred in his eyes. Every time they're out, this happens." Then he meets another neighbor, a tough and pimp called Raymond Sintès. (Sintès was Camus's mother's name.) Sintès asks him if he isn't disgusted by the way the old man treats his dog: "I answered no."

Sintès asks Meursault to eat with him. "It struck me that this would save my having to cook my dinner, so I said, 'Thanks very much.'"

Sintès asks Meursault's advice on a personal matter. He had been keeping a girl who had "let him down," and he wanted to teach her a lesson. He wanted to write her a letter 'with insults in it and at the same time things to make her sorry.' Then when she came back he'd go to bed with her and just when she was 'properly primed up he'd spit in her face and throw her out of the room.' I agreed it wasn't a bad plan; it would punish her all right."

Raymond asks Meursault to write this letter for him, and Meursault agrees. "The moment he mentioned the girl's name, I knew she was a Moor."

Meursault and Marie again go swimming and then to bed. "A moment later she asked me if I loved her. I said that sort of question had no meaning, really; but I supposed I didn't." Then they heard thuds and a scream from Raymond's room. "Marie and I went out to see. The woman was still screaming and Raymond still knocking her about. Marie said, wasn't it horrible! I didn't answer. Then she asked me to go and fetch a policeman, but I told her I didn't like policemen." Raymond is charged with assault, and Meursault agrees to act as his witness. Raymond rings him at the office. "'It's like this,' he said. 'I've been shadowed all morning by some Arabs. One of them's the brother of that girl I had the row with. If you see him hanging round the house when you come back, pass me the word.'

"I promised to do so."

Meursault agrees to marry Marie. "Marie came that evening and asked me if I'd marry her. I said I didn't mind; if she was keen on it, we'd get married. . . .

"Then she remarked that marriage was a serious matter.

"To which I answered: 'No.'"

Meursault gives evidence for Raymond about the girl's having been false to him. The police, without checking Meursault's statement, let Raymond off with a warning. As they leave the police station: "I saw some Arabs lounging against the tobacconist's window. They were staring at us silently, in the way they have [*à leur manière*]—as if we were blocks of stone or dead trees."

Raymond observes that one of them is the brother of the girl whom he has beaten.

They go to the beach, drink and swim. The Arabs follow them.

"I noticed two Arabs in blue dungarees a long way down the beach, coming in our direction. I gave Raymond a look and he nodded, saying, 'That's him.'"

There is a fight on the beach in which one of the Arabs draws a knife, and Raymond is cut on the arm and face.[7] He has his wounds bandaged, and he and Meursault walk along the beach and find the two Arabs.

"The man who had slashed Raymond stared at him without speaking. The other man was blowing down a little reed and extracting from it three notes of the scale, which he played over and over again, while he watched us from the corner of an eye."

Raymond has his revolver, and he and Meursault discuss whether to shoot the Arab who has cut Raymond. Meursault advises against shooting him in cold blood, and Raymond gives Meursault his revolver. "And just then it crossed my mind that one might fire,

[7] Stuart Gilbert's English translation of the fight passage, in the widely read Vintage Books edition of *The Stranger*, uses language not used by Camus. At one point Gilbert has "the native," where the French text simply has "*l'autre*," and at another "the natives" where the text simply has "*ils*."

or not fire—and it would come to absolutely the same thing.

"Then, all of a sudden, the Arabs vanished; they'd slipped backward[8] behind the rock." Raymond goes back, and Meursault walks on the beach in the noonday glare and heat. He finds the Arab on the beach, and the Arab draws his knife.

"Then everything began to reel before my eyes, a fiery gust came from the sea, while the sky cracked in two, from end to end, and a great sheet of flame poured down through the rift. Every nerve in my body was a steel spring, and my grip closed on the revolver. The trigger gave, and the smooth underbelly of the butt jogged my palm. And so, with that crisp, whipcrack sound, it all began. I shook off my sweat and the clinging veil of light. I knew I'd shattered the balance of the day, the spacious calm of this beach on which I had been happy. But I fired four more shots into the inert body, on which they left no visible trace. And each successive shot was another loud, fateful rap on the door of my undoing."

This passage closes the first part of *L'Etranger*. The second part deals with Meursault's trial and sentence. He is told that the police report that he had shown "great callousness" at his mother's funeral, and his lawyer asks him whether he felt grief on "that sad occasion."

"I answered that, of recent years, I'd rather lost the

[8] Gilbert has "slipped like lizards." There is no explicit saurian simile in the original but the verb *se couler* may be taken as suggesting such a comparison.

habit of noting my feelings, and hardly knew what to answer. I could truthfully say I'd been quite fond of Mother—but really that didn't mean much. All normal people, I added as an afterthought, had more or less desired the death of those they loved, at some time or another.

"Here the lawyer interrupted me, looking greatly perturbed.

" 'You must promise me not to say anything of that sort at the trial, or to the examining magistrate.' "

At the trial, the court is indignant at the revelations that he had declined to see his mother's body, that he had smoked cigarettes and slept and drunk *café au lait* in the presence of the body, and that he and Marie had gone to bed together on the day after the funeral. The prosecutor emphasizes Meursault's callousness; the defense pleads homicide with extenuating circumstances and argues that the fact that "for one tragic moment he lost his self-control" should not earn him the death sentence. He is sentenced to death and while awaiting execution he rejects the chaplain's offer of the consolation of religion. "Nothing, nothing had the least importance, and I knew quite well why. He, too, knew why. From the dark horizon of my future a sort of slow, persistent breeze had been blowing toward me, all my life long, from the years that were to come. And on its way that breeze had leveled out all the ideas that people tried to foist on me in the equally unreal years I then was living through. What difference could they make to me, the deaths of others, or a mother's love, or his God; or the way a man decides to live, the fate he thinks he chooses, since one and the same fate was bound to 'choose' not only me but thousands of millions of privileged people who, like him, called themselves my brothers? Surely, surely he must see that? Every man alive was privileged; there was only one class of men, the privileged class. All alike would be condemned to die one day; his turn, too, would come like the others'. And what difference could it make if, after being charged with murder, he were executed because he didn't weep at his mother's funeral, since it all came to the same thing in the end?"

After the chaplain's departure he falls asleep. As he wakes up he hears a steamer's siren. "People were starting on a voyage to a world which had ceased to concern me forever. Almost for the first time in many months I thought of my mother. . . . With death so near, Mother must have felt like someone on the brink of freedom, ready to start life all over again. No one, no one in the world had any right to weep for her. And I, too, felt ready to start life all over again. It was as if that great rush of anger had washed me clean, emptied me of hope, and, gazing up at the dark sky spangled with its signs and stars, for the first time, the first, I laid my heart open to the benign indifference of the universe. To feel it so like myself, indeed, so brotherly, made me realize that I'd been happy, and that I was happy still. For all to be accomplished, for me to feel less lonely, all that remained to hope was that on the day of my execution there should be a huge crowd of spectators and that they should greet me with howls of execration."

Years later, in a preface to an English-language edition of *L'Etranger*, Camus wrote: ". . . the hero of the book is condemned because he doesn't play the game. In this sense he is a stranger to the society in which he lives; he drifts in the margin, in the suburb of private, solitary, sensual life. This is why some readers are tempted to consider him as a waif. You will have a more precise idea of this character, or one at all events in closer conformity with the intentions of the author, if you ask yourself in what way Meursault doesn't play the game. The answer is simple: He refuses to lie. Lying is not only saying what is not true. It is also and especially saying more than is true, and, as far as the human heart is concerned, saying more than one feels. This what we all do every day to simplify life. Meursault, despite appearances, does not wish to simplify life. He says what is true. He refuses to disguise his feelings, and immediately society feels threatened. He is asked, for example, to say that he regrets his crime according to the ritual formula. He replies that he feels about it more annoyance than real regret, and this shade of meaning condemns him.

"Meursault for me is, then, not a waif, but a man who is poor and naked, in love with the sun which leaves no shadows. Far from its being true that he lacks all sensibility, a deep, tenacious passion animates him, a passion for the absolute and for truth. It is a still negative truth, the truth of being and of feeling, but one without which no victory over oneself and over the world will ever be possible.

"You would not be far wrong, then, in reading *The*

Stranger as a story of a man who, without any heroics, accepts death for the sake of truth. I have sometimes said, and always paradoxically, that I have tried to portray in this character the only Christ we deserved. You will understand after these explanations that I said this without any intention of blasphemy and only with the slightly ironic affection which an artist has the right to feel towards the characters whom he has created."

Essentially the same view is taken by many commentators on this novel, and some have gone even further: "Though he [Meursault] does not condemn social oppression, nor tries to fight it, he denounces it through his quiet refusal to conform to the defiant attitudes one expects of him. One realizes that this indifferent man is intractable in his respect for truth. On this point he exhibits a surprising and even heroic firmness since in the end it will cost him his life."[9]

I have found from reading a number of students' essays on Camus that a prevalent stock response is one of seeing Meursault as a hero and martyr for the truth, and at the same time identifying with him.

Yet the Meursault of the actual novel is not quite the same person as the Meursault of the commentaries. Meursault in the novel lies. He concocts for Raymond the letter which is designed to deceive the Arab girl and expose her to humiliation, and later he lies to the police to get Raymond discharged after he has beaten

[9] Rachel Bespaloff, "The World of the Man Condemned to Death," in Germaine Brée (ed.), *Camus: A Collection of Critical Essays* (Englewood Cliffs, N.J., 1962).

the girl up. It is simply not true that Meursault is "intractable in his absolute respect for truth." These episodes show him as indifferent to truth as he is to cruelty. And his consent to these actions sets in motion the chain of events which leads to the killing of the Arab on the beach.

L'Etranger is in fact a more complex and interesting novel than would appear from the commentaries—including Camus's own commentary—which sanctify the hero. There is just one category of phenomena about which Meursault will not lie, and that is his own feelings. Neither to give pleasure to others nor to save them pain nor to save his own skin will he pretend that he feels something that he does not feel. Logically there is no reason why this should be so. There is no reason why he should not use lies to get himself out of the trouble which he got himself into by lies. Indeed, in the second case the motivation is (one could imagine) infinitely stronger than in the first. Yet it is in the second that he resists. The reason can only be that his own feelings, and his feelings about his feelings, are sacrosanct. They are the god whom he will not betray and for whom he is martyred. His integrity is that of the artist, the Nietzschean integrity. The idea of him as an enemy of "social oppression" lacks reality. When Raymond is beating up the Arab girl, Meursault refuses to send for the police because he dislikes the police. But his dislike of the police cannot be dislike of social oppression because he personally makes no move to interrupt the social oppression which is at that moment very tangibly proceeding in Raymond's room as a result of Meursault's letter. The reason why he will not have the police sent for is simply, as always, his rigorous fidelity to the hierarchy of his own feelings. He dislikes the idea of the police. He is indifferent to the beating up of the woman.

The integrity of the artist is what joins Meursault to his creator. In a note in his *Carnets*, Camus wrote: "Three characters went into the composition of *The Stranger*: two men (one of them me) and a woman." And just as Meursault is scrupulous in regard to his own feelings and indifferent to the society around him, so Camus is rigorous in his treatment of the psychology of Meursault—in the novel, not in his retrospective commentaries on it—and lax in his presentation of the society which condemns Meursault to death. In practice, French justice in Algeria would almost certainly not have condemned a European to death for shooting an Arab who had drawn a knife on him and who had shortly before stabbed another European. And most certainly Meursault's defense counsel would have made his central plea that of self-defense, turning on the frightening picture of the Arab with a knife. There is no reference to the use of any such defense or even to the bare possibility of an appeal to European solidarity in a case of this kind. This is as unrealistic as to suppose that in an American court, where a white man was charged with killing a black man who had pulled a knife, the defense counsel would not evoke, or the court be moved by, white fear of blacks. The court is presented as if it were a court in a European town, dealing with an incident involving members of a homogeneous population. The kind of irrelevance and injustice of which it is shown capable is of the same order as in, say, André Gide's *Journal de la Cour d'Assises*: That is to say, a generalized human sentimentality. But the presentation in this way of a court in Algeria trying a crime of this kind involves the novelist in the presentation of a myth: the myth of French Algeria. What appears to the casual reader as a contemptuous attack on the court is not in fact an attack at all; on the contrary, by suggesting that the court is impartial between Arab and Frenchman, it implicitly denies the colonial reality and sustains the colonial fiction. The impression of radical rejection and revolt which so many readers have received from the novel is therefore deceptive because, concealed near its heart, lies the specific social fiction vital to the *status quo* in the place where the novel is set. This fiction does not pervade the novel evenly: what is softened and distorted, by being made noncolonial, is the nature of French rule. For the rest, relations between Europeans and Arabs are not sentimentalized. The Arabs who "were staring at us silently in the way they have—as if we were blocks of stone or dead trees" have nothing in common with the jolly Mediterranean interracialists of Mme. Brée's imagining and of some of Camus's propagandist writing. The tiny phrase *à leur manière* is eloquent in its laconic way, for it includes the colonial "they": the pronoun which needs no antecedent.

L'Etranger had a great success from the date of its

appearance in 1942, and especially in the postwar years. It appears even now to be the best known and most popular of Camus's works among the young. I believe that the main secret of its appeal lies in its combination of a real and infectious joy of living, with a view of society which appears to be, and is not, uncompromisingly harsh. The Meursault one believes in is the Meursault who goes swimming and picks up Marie on the day after his mother died. The obscure feeling that Meursault is right to do this has deep roots. So also has the feeling that he is wrong to do it. It is this sense of its wrongness that is itself put on trial in the trial scene, and it is the sympathy with Meursault, and Meursault's will to live, expressed in the opening scenes, which carries the reader through the unrealities of the court and the strained rhetoric of the scene with the chaplain and the conclusion. Indeed, this is not saying quite enough. It may be that the very unreality of the social setting—made plausible for most readers by exoticism—contributes to the sense of lightness, of freedom, which many readers undoubtedly receive from it. Meursault is living on a borderline between reality and myth: the precise details of the physical setting, and of Meursault's feelings and absences of feeling, derive additional sharpness and immediacy from the dreamlike character of the social setting. The book is like Kafka—whom Camus was reading at this time—but Kafka with major differences. It is Mediterranean and colonial Kafka; Mediterranean in hedonism and *joie de vivre*; colonial in a certain sleight of hand. This last has also

a wider appeal. Albert Memmi points out that the relation of "the colonist who refuses" to the colonial
people resembles, in an exaggerated way, the relation
of left-wing middle-class people to the working class
and the poor generally. In both cases the relation is
generally both abstract and strained, and in both cases
conscious attitudes of sympathy sometimes cover
deeper unconscious layers of suspicion and hostility—
as in current relations of many white liberals to blacks
in America. I have long wondered why so many commentators on *L'Etranger*—including Camus himself—
are so ready to canonize Meursault, granted the
nature of his dealings with the Arab woman and her
brother. A part of the answer certainly lies in the fact
that we feel him to be really tried for the failure to
mourn his mother. Everyone—Meursault himself, the
court, and the author—treats the actual killing and the
sordid transactions which prepare the way for it as
irrelevant. But it is not easy to make the killing of a
man seem irrelevant; in fact it can hardly be done un-
less one is led in some way to regard the man as not
quite a man. And this is what happens. The Europeans
in the book have names—Meursault, Raymond Sintès,
Marie, Salamano, and other minor characters. The
man who is shot has no name, and his relation to the
narrator and his friends is not that of one human being
to another. He looks at them as if they were "blocks of
stone or dead trees." When the narrator shoots down
this blank and alien being and fires "four shots more
into the inert body, on which they left no visible
trace," the reader does not quite feel that Meursault

has killed a man. He has killed an Arab. Both Camus and many of his readers would have been likely to reject that implication with genuine indignation, yet the relative substantiality of Arabs and Europeans in the text carries its own message.

Two critics in the left-wing periodical *France-Observateur* (January 5, 1961) have interested themselves in the European-Arab relation in *L'Etranger*. For Henri Kréa, Meursault's act is "the subconscious realization of the obscure and puerile dream of the 'poor white' Camus never ceased to be." For Pierre Nora, Camus, like other Europeans of Algeria "consciously frozen in historical immobility," was unable to confront the problem of the European-Arab relation, which continued to work in his subconscious: the novel (especially the trial scene) in Nora's belief is "a disturbing admission of historical guilt and takes on the aspect of a tragic anticipation."

The American critic Emmett Parker, author of *Albert Camus: The Artist in the Arena*, treats these suggestions with contempt: "To assume that Camus could only treat the Algerian question on a subconscious level or that he was otherwise incapable of coming to terms with it reveals either Kréa's and Nora's ignorance of a large part of Camus's journalistic writings or their intention deliberately to disregard them." In fact Camus never did come to terms with the situation in question, and his journalistic writings (see below, pp. 77ff.) are the record of his painful and protracted failure to do so. Imaginatively he comes much closer to it, especially in the spacing of certain silences. I believe that while Kréa's interpretation is crude, Nora's is near to the truth.

The relation of European to Arab, unlike the absolute impartiality of the Algiers court, is rooted in reality. It also works in the novel. The faceless Arabs, silently reappearing, help to make us feel the loneliness of the hero. They work like the enigmatic shrouds in Yeats's "Cuchulain Comforted":

Eyes peered out of the branches and were gone.

L'Etranger is partly intended, and has been mainly received, as a statement about the absurdity of mortal life, and some readers will find excessive the emphasis placed here on its social setting and significance. Yet men live and die in particular places and conditions, and their sense of life's meaning, or meaninglessness, derives from their experiences in these places and conditions, and only in these, although its expression will be modified by the language and experience of other men. The extent to which Camus's first novel both precisely reflects in certain parts, and heavily distorts in others, an experience of a colonial situation is therefore not irrelevant. It is, in this critic's opinion, relevant to what rings true in the book, the direct, unsentimentalized experience so tersely evoked in the first half; and to what rings hollow, the artful staging of the trial and the pathos and rhetoric of the prison dialogues. It is also relevant to the future development of his work, as we shall see, and it is relevant to forming an opinion on the role often claimed for Camus, as an expression of the conscience of Western man.[10] We may indeed accept the fact that Camus's work is a notable expression of the Western moral conscience. But we should not ignore the fact that it also registers the hesitations and limitations of that conscience and that one of the great limitations lies along the cultural frontier, in the colony.

Meursault is the contemporary hero of the Absurd: there is also a historical one, Caligula; and a mythological one, Sisyphus.

Caligula, the central figure of Camus's first play, written in 1938 and first performed in 1945, has "a strange look" and a hatred of hypocrisy. He is not identical with Meursault but he springs ultimately from the same stock and from the same general situation. Yet he also is or becomes the situation itself. "Men die and are not happy," he says and becomes the executant of his diagnosis. "Execution," says his faithful slave, Helicon, "relieves and delivers. It is universal, fortifying and just in its applications as well as in its intentions. One dies because one is guilty. One is guilty because one is a subject of Caligula. However, everybody is a subject of Caligula. Therefore everyone is guilty. From which it follows that everyone dies. It is a question of time and patience." Caligula "turns his

[10] John Cruickshank, for example, in a tribute to Albert Camus delivered on January 19, 1960, at the Institut Français, spoke of Camus as "one who in his life and in his work embodied the French moral conscience at its most pure and most persuasive." (John Cruickshank, *Albert Camus and the Literature of Revolt*, New York, 1960.)

philosophy into corpses": he had once wanted to be a just man; in an intolerable world he has found the courage to be pure in evil. He cruelly humiliates the patricians and a slave rejoices:

"Yes, I serve a madman. But you, whom do you serve? Virtue? I'll tell you what I think of that. I was born a slave, so, this tune of virtue, decent man, I learned to dance it under the whip. Caligula did not make speeches to me. He set me free and took me into his palace. That's how I had a chance of taking a look at you, you virtuous people. And I saw that you were a dirty-looking lot, with an unpleasant smell, the sickly smell of people who have never suffered or risked anything. I saw noble-looking clothes, but worn hearts, greedy faces, furtive hands. You judges? You, who set up a virtue shop, who dream of security as a girl dreams of love. . . . You would take on yourselves to judge a man who has suffered beyond all counting . . . ? You'll have to strike me first! Despise the slave Cherea! He is above your virtue since he can still love this wretched master of his and defend him against your noble lies, your perjured mouths."

The young Scipion, who is "pure in good," as Caligula is "pure in evil," finds that something in himself is like Caligula: "The same flame burns our hearts." Even Cherea, who kills Caligula, has had to "silence in myself what could be like him." Basically Cherea's reason for rejecting Caligula is that "I want to live and to be happy. I believe that you can't do either if you push absurdity to its logical conclusions. I am like everyone else."

The reader or the audience is led to feel a certain admiration for Caligula; for his ruthless honesty, his daring, and his style. But as the sequence of his crimes and cruel caprices accumulates, he becomes repulsive, a monster. When at the end he is cut down by Cherea and his fellow conspirators, his last words are felt as a threat: "I am still alive."

There is nothing in *Caligula* corresponding to the strategy whereby we are led in *L'Etranger*—a slightly later work—to sympathize with a much more modest killer. Nor is there anything in *L'Etranger* which corresponds to the positions of Scipion or of Cherea, or, for that matter, of Helicon. The slaves in *L'Etranger* are silent. The differing conventions of the stage and the novel may be partly responsible for this, but there is also a perceptible shift of emphasis which cannot be accounted for in that way. In *Caligula* the idea of carrying truth of feeling—the artist's truth—to its extreme is shown as hideously inhuman. One is reminded of Proudhon's famous saying: "Nero was an artist, a lyric and dramatic artist, a passionate lover of the ideal, a worshiper of the antique, a collector of medals, a tourist, a poet, an orator, a swordsman, a sophist, a Don Juan, a Lovelace, a nobleman full of wit, fancy, and fellow-feeling, overflowing with love of life and love of pleasure. That is why he was Nero."

But in *L'Etranger* a privileged position is implicitly claimed for truth-about-feeling, for the autonomy of the artist. And this claim in turn is staked in a privileged situation: that of the outpost of civilization, the colony which does not say its name. It is as if Caligula, fascinating but odious on the historic European stage, became humdrum, acceptable, and finally endearing under the African sun.

In September 1940, some months after finishing *L'Etranger*, Camus began working on the first part of *Le Mythe de Sisyphe*, a long essay in which he seeks to give philosophical form to the idea, theme, or slogan of the Absurd.

> The gods had sentenced Sisyphus to roll everlastingly a rock to the top of a mountain, from which the rock fell back by its own weight. They thought, reasonably enough, that there is no more terrible punishment than a useless and hopeless work.
>
> If Homer is to be believed, Sisyphus was the wisest and most prudent of mortals. According to another tradition, however, he went in for being a bandit. I see no contradiction in that.

Sisyphus is "the absurd hero . . . both by his passions and by his torment." The strength of Sisyphus lies in the dignified acceptance of his absurd task: "All the silent joy of Sisyphus is there. His destiny belongs to him." And then, in a phrase which has become slightly comical through excess of contemporaneity: "His rock is his thing."

Le Mythe de Sisyphe begins with a discussion of suicide and goes on to the theme of revolt. Its central message is that the true revolt against the absurdity of existence consists not in suicide but in continuing to live. Suicide is "acceptance pushed to its logical extreme." Real revolt consists in "dying unreconciled and not of one's own free will."

As reasoning, this "logic of revolt" reminds one of that logic of submission whereby Thomas Hobbes proves that it is not necessarily idolatrous to pray to a king for "fair weather or for anything which God only can do for us." This is not idolatry, according to Hobbes, "if a King compel a man to it by the terror of death or other great corporal punishment. . . . For the worship which the Sovereign commandeth to be done unto himself by the terror of his laws is not a sign that he that obeyeth him doth inwardly honour him as a god, but that he is desirous to save himself from death or from a miserable life and that which is not a sign of internal honour is no worship and therefore no idolatry." What the apparently divergent reasonings of Hobbes and of Camus have in common is the agility of life defending itself. In each case a rigorous and linear logic, starting from assumptions which the writer at least in theory accepts, points to the acceptance of death, and in each case the writer jumps clear.

Le Mythe de Sisyphe should not be thought of as a philosophical treatise but as the soliloquy of an artist facing the idea of death. He had been seriously ill and contemplated suicide. What is most moving here is a kind of hymn to life, springing up out of despair:

What is left is a destiny of which only the end is predetermined. Apart from this single predetermined fact of death, all, joy or happiness, is freedom. A world remains of which man is the sole master. What had bound him was the illusion of another world. The fact of his thought no longer lies in renouncing itself, but in springing back in images. It finds play—in myths, no doubt—but myths whose entire depth is that of human pain and which are inexhaustible like pain. Not the divine fable which distracts and blinds but the face, the gesture, and the drama of this earth, reflecting a difficult wisdom and a passion which has no tomorrow.

What is most misleading about the writings of this period, and what has been most uncritically accepted, is their presentation as a literature of revolt. Against what is the revolt? There is certainly a rejection of the Christian cosmogony and of the supernatural generally, but this is in no sense a revolt against the values of Camus's culture: it is an acceptance of the word which Nietzsche long before had spread. A metaphysical revolt against a cosmos without God, a revolt taking the form of a decision to continue to live, seems to lack substance. It is true that at least at one point in his writings of this period Camus seems to imply that his version of metaphysical revolt is linked to, or cognate with, social and political revolt. In a section on "Hope and the Absurd in Kafka," which he planned as part of *Le Mythe de Sisyphe* but had to drop under conditions of wartime censorship[11] when the book was published in 1943, he notes that "one may as legitimately interpret Kafka's work in the sense of a social criticism [as well as in terms of supernatural disquiet]. Probably one does not have to choose between these interpretations: they are both valid. In absurd terms, as we have seen, revolt against

[11] Kafka, being a Jew, was not acceptable. Dostoevski took his place.

men is aimed also at God. The great revolutions are always metaphysical."

The part which Camus later played in the Resistance, discussed in the next section, has rendered credible in retrospect the idea of a revolutionary Camus. It would, however, be anachronistic to relate Camus's writing of this period to the Resistance. *Caligula* was finished before the war, *L'Etranger* before the occupation of France. Only *Le Mythe de Sisyphe* (September 1940 to February 1941) can have anything to do with the Resistance, and even then only as reflecting obscurely a movement of ideas preceding the decision to join the Resistance—a decision which seems to have crystallized at the end of 1941.

The real significance, and the source of the appeal, of the work of this period is one not of revolt but of affirmation. To a generation which saw no reason for hope, it offered hope without reason. It offered a category—the Absurd—in which logical, psychological, philosophical, and even social and political difficulties could be encapsulated, and it allowed the joy of being alive, in the presence of death, to emerge. It was neither a revolutionary message nor an especially moral one; but it was a singularly sweet and exhilarating message to a whole generation that was also pleased to think of it as revolutionary and moral. I belonged to that generation, and if I scrutinize that message now with the wary eyes of middle age, I am no less grateful for having received it in my youth.

The Plague

ii

From Lyon, where he lived during the last months of 1940, Camus returned to Algeria in January 1941, and there in Oran, after finishing *Le Mythe de Sisyphe*, he began work on *La Peste* (*The Plague*).

On December 19, 1941, the Germans executed Gabriel Péri. The news of this event was followed by Camus's decision to enter into active resistance. After the war he told an interviewer: "You ask me why I took the side of the Resistance. This is a question which has no meaning for a certain number of men, of whom I am one. It seemed to me, and it still seems to me, that you cannot be on the side of concentration camps. I understood then that I hated violence less than the institutions of violence. and to be quite accurate I remember very well the day when the wave of revolt which was within me reached its climax. It was one morning in Lyon and I was reading in the paper the news of the execution of Gabriel Péri."[1] According to Roger Quilliot, the editor of the well-documented Pléiade Edition of Camus's works, Camus did not like to talk about his life in the Resistance; "he didn't like the 'veteran' style, no doubt from a decent reticence and fidelity to a memory" (*par pudeur et nostalgie*).

In the spring of 1942, following a new attack of tuberculosis, Camus returned to France, where he lived on a farm, Le Panelier, in a village in Auvergne, not far from St. Etienne. He was already involved in underground activity, which took him to St. Etienne and to Lyon—where he bicycled, in spite of his state of health, many miles daily. By 1943 he was a member of the important underground group known as Combat. His wife had returned to Oran in November 1942 and was separated from him as a result of the Allied landings, a situation which is reflected in *La Peste*. He went to Paris in the spring of 1943 and worked openly as a reader for Gallimard while continuing both his clandestine work and his writing. He had begun work on *La Peste*, which was to be published after the war, in 1947. He finished the first draft of his play *Le Malentendu*.[2] And

[1] There seems to be a slip of memory here. Camus left Lyon at the beginning of 1941 and did not return to France until the spring of 1942.

[2] *Le Malentendu* treats the old folk theme of the son who returns without telling his name and is murdered by his brigand parents. The themes of the stranger and of exile or separation are perennial in Camus's work.

in July he wrote the first of his *Lettres à un Ami Allemand*, an underground polemical work. By the autumn of 1943 he was responsible for the publication of *Combat*, the important Resistance newspaper produced by the underground network of the same name. At the Liberation, on August 24, 1944, appeared the first open number of *Combat*, with Camus's name on its masthead as editor-in-chief and his historic editorial, opening with the words: "Paris fires all its bullets into the August night. In this vast setting of stone and water, all round this river heavy with history, the barricades of liberty have risen once more. Once more, justice has to be bought with the blood of men."

The action of *La Peste*—the novel which reflects Camus's experience of occupation and resistance—is set in the Algerian coastal city of Oran, "a town without suspicions, a modern town." The central figure of the story and also the narrator—although his identity as narrator is revealed only at the end—is Dr. Rieux.

On the morning of April 16, Dr. Rieux finds a dead rat on the landing outside his consulting-room. He is preoccupied with other matters: he says good-by to his wife, who suffers from tuberculosis and has to leave for a cure in the mountains. The outbreak of the plague in Oran will cut her off from him—the torment of separation is one of the principal themes of *La Peste*.

A journalist, Rambert, comes to see Rieux. Rambert

has to write a story for one of the big Paris newspapers on living conditions among the Arabs and wants some information from Rieux about their state of health.

Rieux told him that this state was not good. But he wanted to know before going any farther if the journalist could tell the truth.

"Certainly," said Rambert.

"I mean: can you condemn totally?"

"Totally? No, I must admit. But I suppose that total condemnation would be unwarranted."

Gently Rieux said that indeed total condemnation would be unwarranted but that in asking the question he was only trying to find out whether Rambert's testimony could or could not be without reservations.

"Testimony without reservations is the only kind of testimony I accept. I shall therefore not supply information in support of your testimony."

Dead rats are found in increasing numbers:

From dark corners, from basements, from cellars, from sewers, they came up in long tottering lines to stagger at the light, turn round and die near men. . . . You might have thought that the very earth on which our houses stood was purging itself, allowing boils and pus which until then have been at work inside to come to the surface.

An old asthmatic patient of the doctor's rubs his hands and repeats with senile joy, "They are coming out. They are coming out."

The rats decrease in number; finally no more are seen. The concierge of Rieux's apartment building falls ill. He will be the first human victim of the plague. A clerk, Grand, reports the attempted suicide of his neighbor, Cottard. The concierge dies: "Our fellow citizens, as they were now to realize, had never imagined that our little town could be a place specially marked out for rats to die there in the sunshine and for concierges to perish there of outlandish diseases. In this they were in error and their ideas fell to be revised."

Rieux's neighbour, Tarrou, keeps a diary of the progress of the plague, noting such details as the fate of the little old man who used to call cats together in order to spit on them and who loses his role in life on account of the disappearance of the cats, because of the rats, and recovers it again because of the reappearance of the cats after the disappearance of the rats. Rieux, like his fellow citizens, finds it hard to believe in the existence of the plague:

"The great scourge is not made to human measure. You think therefore that the great scourge is unreal, it is a bad dream which will pass. . . . Our fellow citizens . . . went on about their business, they got ready for journeys and they had opinions. How could they have thought of the plague which abolishes the future, traveling, and argument? They thought of themselves as free, and no one will ever be free as long as there are scourges."

Dr. Rieux decides that for him the essential is to do his job well. He gets to know Grand, a clerk at the city hall who keeps him informed of the statistics of the growing death-roll of the plague. Grand's career has been handicapped by his inability to use words which he feels to be unsuitable, such as "rights," on the one hand, or "gratitude," on the other. He is writing a book but never gets beyond the endless redrafting of the first sentence, always in quest of *le mot juste*. He becomes one of the steadiest fighters against the plague.

The state of plague is declared, and the city is in quarantine.

The journalist Rambert feels doubly exiled, from his mistress and from his own country. He begins to lay plans for escape.

The would-be suicide, Cottard, has now started to read right-wing newspapers, to frequent expensive restaurants, and to operate on the black market. He, who had been lonely and frightened in ordinary life, finds himself in his element in the middle of the plague.

Rieux refuses to give Rambert a certificate that might help him to escape from the city. At the same time Rieux feels that Rambert, in his single-minded pursuit of happiness, is perhaps right, and right also in accusing him, Rieux, of living in abstraction: "To fight against abstraction you have to get a little like it."

In the cathedral, before a large congregation, the scholarly Jesuit Paneloux preaches a sermon on the plague, a punishment for the sins of the city. The plague is a flail[3] separating the human wheat from the chaff. Father Paneloux develops the moving image of the flail: "The great wooden implement turning above

[3] The French word *fléau*, used metaphorically in the sense of scourge, has the basic meaning of "flail." The word *fléau*, which in its metaphorical sense is of course applicable to both "plague" and "war" and serves as a conceptual link between them, is used repeatedly throughout the novel.

the city, 'striking at random and rising bloodstained, scattering blood and human pain, for a sowing which would prepare the harvests of truth.' "

The statistics of the plague, considered too disquieting in their weekly form, are now broadcast as daily figures. Grand is troubled by the problem of conjunctions. Rambert looks for people who can help him get away. Tarrou helps to form an organization of plague-fighters. Rieux and Tarrou exchange confidences about their motives. For Rieux the motive is "more or less" his idea of his job, combined with his inability to get used to seeing people die. For him the plague is an interminable defeat. Tarrou asks, " 'Who taught you all that, Doctor?' The reply came immediately: 'Poverty.' " (The French word, *la misère*, is stronger than the English "poverty" but more common than the English "destitution." Camus used it to describe the conditions of his own childhood.)

Rieux asks Tarrou:

"What pushes you into taking a hand in all this?"
"I don't know. My ethic perhaps."
"And what's that?"
"Understanding."

Grand in his off-duty hours continues to work in the hospital as if he were in city hall and tries not to think about the "fair equestrienne" who is the heroine of the eternally unfinished first sentence of his masterpiece. The narrator says that if his story has to have a hero, he would offer Grand: "This dim and insignificant hero whose only merits were a little kindness in his heart and an apparently ridiculous ideal. This will give truth its due, making two and two make four, and give heroism the secondary place which belongs to it, just after, and never before, a generous insistence on happiness. This will also give this chronicle its character, which should be that of a story made with good feelings, that is to say feelings which are neither obviously bad nor uplifting in the contemptible style of the theater."

Rambert learns that Rieux too is separated by the plague from the person he loves. Rambert joins Rieux's plague-fighting organization "until he can find a way to leave the city."

The changing arrangements for the burial of the victims of the plague are set out in detail: "For nothing is less spectacular than a scourge and, by reason of their very duration, great misfortunes are monotonous. In the memory of those who lived them, the terrible days of the plague did not appear as great sumptuous cruel flames, but rather as an endless trampling, crushing everything in its way."

Tarrou tries to understand Cottard and to draw him away from his position of supporting the plague: "There was no use my telling him that the only way not to be separated from others was after all to have a clear conscience. He looked at me nastily and said, 'At that rate no one is ever with anybody.' And then, 'You can say what you like, I'm telling you. The only way to get people together is to send them the plague. Look around you.'"

Orpheus and Eurydice is staged at the municipal

opera house. In the third act the singer who plays Orpheus collapses with the plague. The audience rushes towards the exits.

Cottard and Tarrou remained alone in the auditorium, watching one of the images of what made up their life at that time. The plague on the stage in the form of the twisted body of an actor and in the auditorium a now useless luxury in the form of forgotten fans and lace trailing over the red plush of the seats.

Rambert, who continues his intermittent efforts to leave the city, is surprised that Rieux not only does nothing to stop him but actually seems to encourage him.

"Why tell me to hurry in these circumstances?"
Rieux smiled. "Perhaps because I too want to do something for happiness."

Rambert, however, finally decides to remain in the plague-stricken city because he would be ashamed if he left. Rieux tells him that there is nothing to be ashamed of in preferring happiness.

"Yes," said Rambert, "but there may be something to be ashamed of in being happy by oneself."
Tarrou . . . pointed out that if Rambert wished to share the unhappiness of men he would never have time again for happiness. He would have to choose.
"It's not that," said Rambert. "I always thought that I was a stranger in this town and that I had nothing to do with you. But now that I have seen what I have seen, I know that I belong to this place whether I like it or not. This business concerns us all."

The child of the pompous and self-righteous Judge Othon catches the plague and dies. Othon too joins the organization for fighting the plague. After the child's death, Rieux turns on the priest Paneloux: "That one at least was innocent, and you know it." Shaken, the priest says, "Perhaps we should love what we cannot understand." Rieux says no. "I have a different conception of love and I will always refuse to love a creation in which children are tortured."

Paneloux tells Rieux that he now understands what is called grace.

Paneloux preaches his second sermon to a much smaller congregation. He tells the story of the great plague of Marseille when, out of eighty-one monks at the Convent of Mercy, only four survived the fever, and of these four, three fled. His thought went out to the man who had remained alone in spite of seventy-seven corpses and especially in spite of the example of his three brothers. "And Father Paneloux cried out: 'My brothers, it is necessary to be the one who stays.' "

Paneloux himself falls ill; his disease presents some but not all the classical symptoms of the plague. He clutches his crucifix and dies. "Amid the tumult of fever, Paneloux kept his indifferent look, and when, on the following morning, he was found dead, hanging half out of his bed, his face expressed nothing. On his index card they wrote the words: 'A doubtful case.' "

The graph of the plague begins to flatten out. One of Rieux's colleagues, Richard, finds this development extremely encouraging. He then catches the plague himself and dies "on the level stretch of the graph."

Tarrou tells Rieux the story of his childhood and of his father, a prosecuting attorney, who was an authority on railway timetables. Young Tarrou admired his father until one day he heard him in court calling for the death penalty. Because of his horror of the death penalty, Tarrou became a political militant but comes to realize that in his militancy he himself became a plague-bearer:

"I learned that I had indirectly supported the deaths of thousands of men. That I had even urged on their death by approving the actions and the principles which were certain to produce it. . . . I am ashamed of having been a murderer in my town." At the same time he realized that "even those who were better than others could not save themselves today from killing or allowing people to be killed because it was in the logic of their situation and that we could not make a move in this world without running the risk of killing. 'Yes, I continued to be ashamed. I learned that, that we were all in the plague and I lost peace.'" As for himself, "From the moment in which I refused to kill I condemned myself to a definitive exile. It will be the others who will make history." The only thing that interests him is to know how one becomes a saint. "Can you be a saint without God? This is the only concrete problem that I know today."

Rieux says he prefers to be a man rather than a saint, and Tarrou says, "Yes, we are looking for the same thing, but I am less ambitious."

After these exchanges, Rieux and Tarrou go swimming. Grand falls ill of the plague and is the first victim to recover. The graph of the plague begins to drop. With the beginning of the return of normality, the old services start up again, including the police. Two men appear, looking for Cottard.

The plague, though in decline, still strikes. Tarrou falls ill and dies in Rieux's apartment.

The doctor did not know if in the end Tarrou had found peace but at this moment at least he thought he knew there would no longer be any possible peace for himself, any more than there is an armistice for a mother whose son has been amputated from her or for the man who buried his friend. . . . All that man could win in the game of plague and life was knowledge and memory. Perhaps it was that that Tarrou called "winning."

On the following day Dr. Rieux receives the news of the death of his wife.

The plague is declared over. The gates of the city are opened. Rambert's mistress comes to join him; we are given to understand that their happiness together will not last long.

In the joy of deliverance in the streets, men and women locked in one another's arms affirmed . . . with all the triumph and the injustice of happiness that the plague was over and that terror had had its day. They quietly denied, against all the evidence that we had ever known, that crazy world in which the death of a man was as everyday as that of a fly, that well-defined savagery, that calculated delirium, that imprisonment which carried with it a terrible liberty in relation to everything which was not the present, that smell of death which stupefied all those it did not kill. They denied finally that we had been that stunned people, a part of which every day, stuffed in the snout of a furnace, evaporated in greasy smoke,[4] while the other, loaded with the chains of impotence and fear, awaited its turn.

These were happy for a time at least. They knew now that if there is one thing which one can always desire, and sometimes find, it is human affection.

For all those, on the other hand, who had addressed themselves above man, to something which they did not even imagine, there had been no answer. . . . And Rieux . . . thought that it was right that at least from time to time joy should come to reward those who content themselves with man and with his poor and terrible love.

Dr. Rieux, in his conclusion, acknowledges that he is the narrator and explains his method:

He was well placed to report what he had seen and heard, but he wished to do this with the appropriate restraint. Generally speaking, he set himself not to report more than he had seen, not to attribute to his companions of the plague thoughts which they did not necessarily think, and he used only the documents which chance or misfortune put in his hands. Being called to testify on the occasion of a sort of crime, he retain a certain reserve, as befits a witness of good-will.

Cottard, deprived of the plague, goes mad and starts shooting at people in the street. He kills a dog. The police catch him and beat him.

[4] The direct reference is to mass cremation of the plague victims.

Grand decides to remove all the adjectives from his eternal sentence.

An old patient of Rieux's grumbles: "These people say 'It's the plague—we've had the plague.' A little more and they'd want to be decorated. But what does that mean—the plague? It's life, that's all."

Finally Rieux records his own decision to write the story.

So as not to be one of those who are silent, so as to testify in favor of these victims of the plague, so as to leave at least a memory of the injustice and the violence which were done to them, and so as to tell simply what one learns among scourges, that there are in men more things to be admired than to be despised.

Yet he knew that this chronicle could not be one of outright victory. It could only be the testimony of what had to be done and of what no doubt would have to be accomplished again, against terror and its un-wearying arm, by men who, not being able to be saints and refusing to accept scourges, try, in spite of their personal inner conflicts, to be doctors.

Hearing the cries of joy coming up from the city, Rieux remembered that this joy was always threatened. For he knew what that joyous crowd did not know, and yet can be read in books, that the bacillus of the plague never dies or disappears, that it can remain for tens of years dormant in furniture and linen, that it is waiting patiently in bedrooms, cellars, trunks, handkerchiefs and bundles of paper, and that perhaps the day would come when, for the misfortune and the instruction of men, the plague would wake up its rats again and send them off to die in a happy city.

La Peste is not so much a novel as a sermon in the form of a fable. There are really only three characters: the narrator, the city, and the plague. The personages named in the narrative have little more than symbolic value, the degree of existence required by figures in a morality play, only rarely tinged with some such "humor" as Grand's scrupulous literary ambition.

The narrator, who is one of the principal characters, is hardly Dr. Rieux. The final "disclosure" that Rieux is the narrator does not fully convince us, for the Rieux of the story could hardly have told the story— for one thing he would have been too busy with his practice. It is true that the tone of the narrative— slightly stilted, consciously didactic, and at times verging on the pompous—recurrently suggests the conversation of a provincial doctor. But this pretense is not consistently maintained. This narrator has at his disposal resources of eloquence and irony which do not seem to belong to Dr. Rieux. Yet we are conscious of an individual accent, conscious of being addressed about a personal and deeply significant experience. But Dr. Rieux—always something of a lay figure— gets shouldered aside. It is Albert Camus who is talking to us. This is more than just an ordinary breakdown of the narrator-author substitution in novel-writing. This is not a novel. It is an allegorical sermon[5]—Paneloux's two efforts are sermons within a sermon, setting off the superior quality and content of

[5] "A tract," Camus once called it.

the sermon which encloses them. If we are to be moved by a sermon, we must be moved by the personality and life of the preacher, as well as by his words. And we are in fact moved by the personality and life of Albert Camus through the symbols of his experience. Rieux and Tarrou, standing for the effort and sacrifice of the Resistance, are in a sense guarantors of the sermon, but Camus is the preacher.

The device of making Rieux the narrator, combined with the claim to realism implied by his reliance on Tarrou's notebooks and other documents, is unsatisfactory and even confusing. If the narrator had remained anonymous to the end, the narrative/sermon would have retained its own kind of integrity and the reader would not have been troubled with the question of what the narrator's imaginary documentary sources might conceivably be. I suspect that here Camus was influenced, unhappily, by certain doctrines laid down by Jean-Paul Sartre a few years before as to what "a true novel" had to be. In a true novel, Sartre had said, "as in the world of Einstein, there is no place for a privileged observer."[6] Sartre had attacked Mauriac for ignoring this supposed law and choosing "divine omniscience and omnipotence." "God," Sartre had

[6] *"François Mauriac et la Liberté,"* in *Nouvelle Revue Française,* February 1939. As regards Einstein and literary endeavor, Simone de Beauvoir tells an interesting anecdote, the implications of which Sartre might have profitably pondered. The poet Paul Valéry wished to learn from Einstein how he kept a record of his ideas. Did he keep a notebook? No. Did he write them down on his cuffs? No. How then? Einstein explained that he hardly ever had any ideas—just one or two in his whole lifetime.

concluded, "is not an artist; neither is M. Mauriac." Mauriac himself was so impressed by this nonsense that in his next novel, *La Pharisienne*, he put in a quantity of diaries, testaments, and confessions, thus rebutting the charge of omniscience. The final avowal of the narrator of *La Peste* also has the effect of making the novel apparently conform to Sartre's requirements for a true novel. He is not a privileged observer, because he has made it his aim not to report more things than he has actually been able to see. He explicitly disavows any claim to omniscience, since he aims "not to lend to his companions of the plague year thoughts which they did not necessarily think." By qualifying as a "true novel," *La Peste* unfortunately moved a little away from its own true nature, which was not that of a novel at all.

If the justificatory device of the revelation of the identity of the narrator be ignored, the actual character of the sermon stands out more clearly and its great force is more directly felt.

It is the author who, through the intermediary of only token personages, to whom his "godlike" relation is only thinly dissimulated, is at grips with the city and the plague. The city of Oran in *La Peste* is of course a symbol for France under the Occupation (as well as, more diffusely, for man's condition). It is also, but with rather disconcerting intermissions, the city of Oran, with its own specific characteristics, under the impact of an imagined plague. Certain consequences of the plague enable Camus to make life in Oran more like life in Lyon or Paris and deprive it of Algerian particularism. Thus the plague cuts Oran off from the sea, which for Camus is a special and some-how sanctifying part of the Algerian experience.[7] Yet puzzling features remain, and these tend to correspond to puzzling features of *L'Etranger*.

The occasion on which Rieux first demonstrates the rigorous character of his own integrity is in response to questions put to him by the journalist Rambert about health conditions among the Arabs. This is before the plague has declared itself. When Rieux learns that Rambert would not be in a position to "condemn totally" the health situation among the Arabs, should he find that it deserved such condemnation—which in Rieux's own belief it does not—he refuses to give him any information on the subject. Now the curious thing is that, after having provided the occasion for this demonstration of integrity, the Arabs of Oran abso-lutely cease to exist. Their problems, including their health problems, had been sufficiently large and dis-tinct to attract the visit of a reporter from "a large Paris newspaper," but at that point they disappear. Not only are all the named characters Europeans—as in *L'Etranger*—but even the silent, nameless, faceless Arabs of *L'Etranger* have departed. Their houses re-main, and that is all. The only reference even to them is in one small scene where Rambert calls on Rieux for the second time to ask his help in order to get out of the city. Rambert reminds Rieux that he called on him before to ask him for "information on the living conditions of the Arabs."

[7] The occasion when Rieux and Tarrou go swimming is an exceptional and privileged case: they have passes.

" 'Yes,' said Rieux. 'Well, you have a fine subject for reporting on now.' " By this time, of course, the plague has broken out.

Rambert accompanies Rieux on a journey to a downtown dispensary. "They went down through the alleys of the native quarter (*quartier nègre*).[8] It was almost dusk, but the town, once so noisy at that hour, seemed curiously deserted. Only a few trumpet calls in the still golden sky showed that the military were still pretending to carry on their business. During this time, along the steep streets between the blue, ocher and violet walls of the Moorish houses, Rambert talked with great excitement."

"Curiously deserted" indeed. Neither Rieux, the doctor, nor Rambert, the reporter, ever goes into these houses. We hear nothing of the progress of the plague among them. The Arab question is simply abolished, once it has served to reveal the differing standards of two Europeans.[9] Up to a point, the strategy of the fable requires the disappearance of the Arabs. It was

---

[8] "There is in Oran a district which was sometimes called *le village nègre*. Why the name? I don't know, for there are probably as many black people there as there are Swiss in the Swiss Village in Paris—that's to say, not many. . . . The majority of the inhabitants of the district are Algerian Moslems." My informant, M. Jean Denis, was born in the *village nègre*, which had its European population also.

[9] The only other reference in *La Peste* to the continued existence of Arabs occurs when the criminal Cottard takes fright at the remark made by a tobacconist about a report from Algiers on "a young clerk who had killed an Arab on a beach." The tobacconist's remark might be described as bourgeois but interracial: "If they put all that riffraff in prison, decent people might be able to breathe."

metropolitan France, not Algeria, which was occupied by the Germans. In the story of occupation and resistance there was not any factor, directly involved, corresponding to the Arab population of Algeria. Myths and fables require a certain simplification, and it is therefore not surprising that Arabs should be kept out of the picture. What is surprising and disquieting, on the contrary, is that the subject of their existence in the setting of the city should be introduced—in a context of rigorous insistence on the whole truth—as a preliminary to the story of a city in which they have no existence, and in which only the local color of the façades of their houses remains. This is a very serious flaw in the book, because it destroys the integrity of the conception of one of the central characters: the city itself. The city becomes a "never was" city, whereas we should be able to think of it as a real city under an imagined plague.

The difficulty derives, I believe, from the whole nature of Camus's relation to the German occupiers, on one hand, and to the Arabs of Algeria on the other. It comes natural to him, from his early background and education, to think of Oran as a French town and of its relation to the plague as that of a French town to the Occupation. But just below the surface of his consciousness, as with all other Europeans in Africa, there must have lurked the possibility of another way of looking at things—an extremely distasteful one. There were Arabs for whom "French Algeria" was a fiction quite as repugnant as the fiction of Hitler's new European order was for Camus and his friends. For such Arabs, the French were in Algeria by virtue of the same right by which the Germans were in France: the right of conquest. The fact that the conquest had lasted considerably longer in Algeria than it was to last in France changed nothing in the essential resemblance of the relations between conquerer and conquered. From this point of view, Rieux, Tarrou, and Grand were not devoted fighters against the plague: they were the plague itself.

Camus would, of course, never have accepted this analogy as just, and it may well be that at this time he was not even conscious that anyone could make such an analogy.[10] Yet there was a sense in which the force of the analogy thrust itself on him. It just was not possible to think of Arabs generally as feeling about German domination over Frenchmen as Frenchmen generally felt about that. It therefore was not possible to include them in a fable about Frenchmen under occupation. Since he wanted to situate his fable in a city which he knew, Oran, and since that city contained a large Arab population, these Arabs had to be removed in order to make that notionally French city a really French one. At the same time, Camus's position does not permit him to look coolly and analytically at the reasons why the Arabs have to be got out of the picture. He therefore leaves them out without admitting

[10] After the war he recognized at least one aspect of the analogy. Writing of repression and torture in Madagascar and Algeria he wrote: "Yet the fact is there, clear and hideous as truth: we are doing, in these cases, what we blamed the Germans for doing." (*Combat*, May 10, 1947; in *Actuelles I.*) See below, pp. 78–79.

that he is leaving them out. Their streets, even if they are "curiously deserted,"[11] and their houses—or at least the fronts of them—are still there. It is astonishing that this great evasion should be preceded by a homily on the need for total honesty about a situation which is then passed over in total silence. It is also surprising—though less so—that commentators on Camus have missed the significance of this artistic final solution of the problem of the Arabs of Oran. Most European criticism, ethnocentric to the point of imagining itself universal, slides easily into colonial assumptions and perspectives and notices the appearance of "politics" only when these assumptions and perspectives are contested.[12] Together with the Arabs, the "settler" characteristics of the European inhabitants have to be left out. In a 1939 essay, "Le Minotaure ou la Halte d'Oran,"[13] Camus describes Oran's Settler House (La Maison du Colon), with its mosaics showing "a gracious settler, with a bow tie and a solar topee, receiving the homage of a procession of slaves in classical dress" (he adds in a footnote: "Another quality of the Algerian race [sic] is, as you can see, candor"). There is no Settler House in the Oran of La Peste, and no equivalent to what it represents.

[11] Some forty pages farther on, Tarrou's notebook, describing conditions in the city generally, tells of the crowded streets in the evenings, at a slightly later period. These crowded streets are European.
[12] Looking through the index of a representative English work on Camus, I found an entry under "Afterlife, the," but none under "Arabs."
[13] In Quilliot, Albert Camus: Essais (Paris, 1965).

The city is partly unreal; the plague is entirely convincing, and so is the narrator's relation to it. Camus here seems to have fused his experience of tuberculosis and of occupation. The deliberate sobriety with which he chronicles the progress of this abstract destroyer carries extraordinary conviction. It is probable that no direct account of the Occupation could have conveyed the essence of its horror so well as does this story, by its depersonalization of the enemy. Later, in his dramatic treatment of the same theme in *L'Etat de Siège*, Camus was to turn the plague into a person, the character of a dictator. The extent to which the power of the fable shrinks under this treatment is a measure of the importance of the impersonal in *La Peste*. It is only when the plague is in decline that the narrator begins to refer to it in human terms, with overtones of a contemptuous but faintly nostalgic pity, curiously recalling the terms in which Mauriac's narrator chronicles the decline into humanity of that female scourge Brigitte Pian.

Seeing the plague miss prey which seemed intended for it, seeing it intensify in certain districts for two or three days, while it disappeared from certain others, seeing it multiply its victims on Monday and Wednesday letting them almost all go, seeing it in this way, getting out of breath or rushing on, you would have said that it was losing control through nervous tension and weariness, that it was losing, as well as its dominion over itself, the sovereign and mathematical efficiency which had been its strength. . . . It seemed that the plague itself was at bay and that its sudden weakness gave new force to the blunted weapons which had been used against it up to then.

The impersonal character of the destroyer and the abstractions necessary for its apprehension serve to make life itself more vivid and tangible. The characters in the story are not themselves particularly human, but their struggles with the plague are human. One might almost say "desperately human," but in fact this would be wrong. This is not a novel of desperation but a sermon of hope. And, as in all Camus's best work, there is beneath all the overt horror a deep sense of the joy of life. The almost unremitting grimness of the narrative is subtly transformed by a current of dry, crisp gaiety in the prose. This tension between what is said and how it is said gives *La Peste* an extraordinarily haunting quality; it is one of those rare books that have the capacity to transform the reader's imaginative world so that henceforward the plague-stricken city becomes an aspect of his environment.

With all its flaws, *La Peste* is a masterpiece: not a great novel, but a great allegorical sermon. And there is a sense in which the gravest of its flaws—the ill-disguised suppression of a profoundly relevant truth about the city of the plague—gives an additional tragic resonance to the work. *La Peste* ends, like *Caligula*, with a warning: the bacillus of the plague can lie dormant for years "in furniture and linen" and may again one day "waken its rats and send them to die in a happy city."

Eight years after the publication of *La Peste*, the rats came up to die in the cities of Algeria.[14] To apply another of Camus's metaphors, the Algerian insurrection was "the eruption of the boils and pus which had before been working inwardly in the society." And this eruption came precisely from the quarter in which the narrator had refused to look: from the houses which Dr. Rieux never visited and from the conditions about which the reporter Rambert never carried out his inquiry.

The realization of this adds a new dimension to the sermon. The source of the plague is what we pretend is not there, and the preacher himself is already, without knowing it, infected by the plague.

[14] In "Albert Camus's Algeria" (in Germaine Brée [ed.], *Camus: A Collection of Critical Essays*, [Englewood Cliffs, N.J., 1962]) R. Quilliot writes of "the rats of colonialism, an old sickness that was dragging on in Algeria." M. Quilliot seems, however, like Camus himself, to think that "colonialism" could in some way be eradicated without France's having to leave Algeria.

The Fall

iii

During the first three years after the liberation,
Camus was the most brilliant and the most influential figure on the non-Communist Left in
France, and his fame spread through Europe
and the United States.

L'Etranger and *Le Mythe de Sisyphe*, both
published during the war by Gallimard, had
been much discussed, mainly in terms of the
pessimism and nihilism attributed to them, so
that Camus's name was already well known in
literary circles when the first "open" number
of *Combat*, with his name as editor-in-chief,
brought the revelation of his Resistance role.
He continued to edit *Combat* until June 1947.
His reputation as a writer grew through the
success on the stage of *Caligula* with Gérard
Philippe (September 1945) and the immediate
success of *La Peste* on its publication in June

1947.[1] Many critics reviewed *La Peste* in terms of "godless holiness" (*sainteté laïque*), and Camus personally came to be identified as the model of the just man. Although he repudiated any such identification, it has continued as a central element in his fame.[2]

Politically, the period during which Camus continued to edit *Combat* was that of the coalition of Resistance forces, which resembled in some ways the prewar Popular Front. It was not until May 1947, when Paul Ramadier dismissed the Communist members of his cabinet, that the Cold War really struck France. Camus's tenure as editor of the "open" *Combat* therefore coincides almost exactly with the postwar, pre-Cold War period.

In the early post-liberation months, Camus's *Combat* favored the carrying through of a social revolution by the triumphant Resistance. The content of the revolution was never very clearly defined, and the whole concept was seriously qualified quite early: "If tomorrow the people of France, called upon to express themselves freely, repudiated the policies of the Resistance, the Resistance would yield" (October 8, 1944).[3]

[1] Two other plays, *Le Malentendu* (1945) and *L'Etat de Siège* (1948), were unsuccessful on the stage.

[2] See, for example, a book by Georges Hourdin entitled *Camus le Juste*, published in 1962 in the collection *Tout le Monde en Parle*. In England, and especially in America, this identification is even more solidly established.

[3] *Actuelles I* (Paris, 1950). Such of Camus's journalism as he wished to preserve was collected in the three volumes *Actuelles I, II,* and *III*; the third volume has the subtitle *Chroniques Algériennes*. Additional articles by Camus are included in R. Quilliot's Pléiade edition as *Textes Complémentaires*.

There was, however, one area in which the idea of revolution had a reasonably precise content, and that was the area of revolutionary justice: the death penalty for wartime collaborators. Here, in the first months, Camus's *Combat* and the Communists are united on a Jacobin line. "This country," wrote Camus on September 11, 1944, "does not need a Talleyrand. It needs a Saint-Just." Camus himself was compared to Saint-Just at this time. Following a controversy with François Mauriac—in which Camus later agreed that Mauriac was right—and because of increasing uneasiness about how the purges were being conducted, Camus began to modify his position. In January 1945 he came out—with one of those double negatives that were to become increasingly characteristic of his political style—"against both hatred and amnesty." By August 1945 he found that the purges had become "odious." In November 1946 he published an important series of articles in *Combat* under the title "Ni Victimes ni Bourreaux" ("Neither Victims nor Executioners"). In these articles—the essential themes of which would later be further developed in *L'Homme Révolté*—Camus's reaction against violence took a specifically anti-Communist turn: "The Communists are logically consistent with the very principles and the irrefutable dialectic which the socialists nonetheless want to keep." Here, just on the verge of the open Cold War split, Camus first expresses an idea that will become an obsession with him and with many others during the Cold War period: the idea that violence and lies have in some special sense their home among the Communists because there they are legitimized by a philosophy of history. In the liberal West, on the other hand, though violence and lies occur, they are not justified by a philosophy of history. Thus Western violence and Eastern violence take on a different moral significance, requiring a different moral response.

Two years earlier, Camus had written: "If we are in agreement neither with the philosophy of Communism, nor with its practical ethic, we vigorously reject political anti-Communism because we know what inspires it and what are its undeclared objectives" (October 7, 1944). By the end of 1946, however—and increasingly thereafter—he grew to forget his original distrust of "political anti-Communism," and his increasingly articulate and emphatic hostility to Communist philosophy turned into political anti-Communism. The full significance of "neither victims nor executioners" did not become clear until later, with the publication of *L'Homme Révolté* and the break with Jean-Paul Sartre (1951–1952). In the intervening period it seemed not so much that Camus had taken a definite side in the Cold War but that, like Sartre and others, he was trying to find a median position, separate from both Communists and Gaullists in French politics, and opposed to siding with either of the great blocs then beginning their confrontation in international politics. He gave some support in the spring of 1948 to Sartre's neutralist *Rassemblement Démocratique Révolutionnaire* but did not actually join it. During 1949 and 1950—a period in which his health suffered a relapse—he was working on the long philosophical essay *L'Homme Révolté*, which appeared in October 1951. His play *Les Justes*, which opened in Paris in December 1949, stood in much the same relation to *L'Homme Révolté* as did *Caligula* to *Le Mythe de Sisyphe*.

The declared purpose of *L'Homme Révolté* is to develop, in relation to murder and revolt, a train of thought which began around suicide and the notion of the absurd. This suggests that *L'Homme Révolté* is a kind of continuation of *Le Mythe de Sisyphe*, and so in a sense it is. In a much more direct sense, however, it is a continuation of "Ni Victimes ni Bourreaux." It is, unlike *Le Mythe de Sisyphe*, a political book and the expression of a political choice.

The central argument of the very long first part of *L'Homme Révolté* resembles that of Yeats's short poem "The Great Day."

> Hurrah for revolution and more cannon-shot!
> A beggar upon horseback lashes a beggar on foot.
> Hurrah for revolution and cannon come again!
> The beggars have changed places, but the lash
>   goes on.

Camus, unlike Yeats, approves the revolt of the beggar on foot. What he wishes to reject is the continuation of the lash, and more especially the justification of the lash in terms of the philosophy of history, the superman or the dictatorship of the proletariat. As in "Ni Victimes ni Bourreaux," the thrust of this argument is against Communists and Communism. Since his argument is aimed not at the lash itself but at systems which he defines as justifying the lash, the Western world largely escaped his censure.[4] Communism, on the other hand, is bracketed with Nazism, but seen as more ambitious, systematic, and dangerous: "Fascism," according to Camus, "never really aspired to a universal empire."

> Russian Communism, on the other hand, because of its very origins, openly aspires to world empire. That is its strength, the depth of its thought, and its importance in our history. . . . For the first time in history, a doctrine and a movement, relying on an armed empire, aims at definitive revolution and the final unification of the world.
>
> This kind of revolution would be the negation of revolt in its original basic sense: Revolt has become the alibi of new tyrants.

The two concluding sections of *L'Homme Révolté* are sharply different. The penultimate section, "Révolte et Art," contains some of Camus's best and most revealing writing. Especially significant for an interpretation of Camus's life and work is the following passage: "The revolutionary spirit, born of total negation, felt instinctively that there was in art, as well as refusal, a consent: that contemplation was in danger of outweighing action, beauty, injustice, and that in certain cases, beauty was in itself an injustice against which there was no appeal." The style of *L'Homme Révolté*, which is that of a highly self-conscious art-

---

[4] Not entirely. Colonial atrocities, including those committed in Algeria in 1945, are mentioned in a footnote.

ist, has therefore its counterrevolutionary implications. Hostile critics were to perceive this clearly. The peroration of *L'Homme Révolté*, "La Pensée de Midi" ("The Thought of Noon"), is in Camus's most lamentable Mediterranean-solar-myth vein: "At the noon of thought the rebel thus refuses divinity in order to share a common struggle and destiny. We will choose Ithaca, the faithful earth, daring and frugal thought, lucid action, the generosity of the man who knows." Nietzsche, Marx, Lenin "can live again indeed . . . but on the understanding that they correct one another and that a limit, in the sun, confines them all."[5]

The action of the play *Les Justes* is set in Russia in 1905. A group of terrorists plot the assassination of an archduke. Most of the terrorists are troubled by the nature of their work, by the problem of having to engage in deceit and violence for the future good of man. One of them, however, has come to cherish the methods more than the ultimate aim:

VOINOV: I can't get used to lying, that's all.

STEPAN: Everybody lies. To lie well—that's the thing.

The poet, Kaliayev, and Stepan are opposed and contrasted:

KALIAYEV: You don't know me, brother. I love life, I am not bored. I joined the revolution because I love life.

[5] Anyone who wants to compare the different kinds of nonsense which can be perpetrated by excellent writers when they take to wallowing in their own idea of their own culture should compare the peroration of *L'Homme Révolté* with that of *Armies of the Night* by Norman Mailer.

STEPAN: I don't love life, but justice, which is above life.

It is Kaliayev who is chosen to throw the bomb at the archduke. He discusses his task with Dora, who has longer experience of the terrorist organization:

KALIAYEV: I love beauty, happiness! That is why I hate despotism. How can I explain it to them? The revolution of course! But revolution for life, to give life a chance, you understand?

DORA (*with enthusiasm*): Yes. . . . (*In a lower voice, after a pause*): And yet we are going to inflict death.

KALIAYEV: Who? Us? Oh you mean . . . It's not the same thing. Oh no, it's not the same thing. And then we are killing to build a world in which no one will ever kill. We accept criminality for ourselves in order that the earth may at last be full of innocent people.

DORA: And if that was not so?

KALIAYEV: Be quiet. You know well that's impossible. Stepan would be right then, and one would have to spit in the face of beauty.

Kaliayev has an opportunity to throw the bomb but refrains from doing so when he sees that the archduke is accompanied by his wife and children. The other terrorists, with the exception of Stepan, approve his decision. It is decided that Kaliayev will make a second attempt. On the eve of the second attempt:

DORA: Tell me one thing: Would you love me if I were not in the organization?

KALIAYEV: Where would you be then?

DORA: I remember when I was a student I used to laugh—I was beautiful then. I used to spend hours walking and dreaming. Would you love me if I were frivolous and careless?

KALIAYEV (*hesitating, and then in a very low voice*): I am dying to tell you: Yes.

DORA (*crying out*): Then say yes, my darling, if you think it and if that is true. Yes, in the face of justice, of poverty and the oppressed people. Yes, yes, I beg of you, in spite of the agony of children, in spite of those who are being hanged and those who are being flogged to death . . .

At the second opportunity, Kaliayev throws his bomb, kills the archduke, and is arrested. In prison he draws away from the warden, Foka, on finding that Foka has also other duties:

KALIAYEV: Then you are an executioner?

FOKA: Yes, sir. And you?

A visitor, Skouratov, identifies himself as a police superintendent. Kaliayev calls him a lackey.

SKOURATOV: At your service. But if I were in your shoes I wouldn't give myself such airs. You will come round perhaps. One begins by wanting justice and one ends by organizing a police force. . . .

The widow of the archduke visits Kaliayev in his cell and tries to convert him to Christianity, but he refuses. He also refuses to betray his comrades. He is sentenced to death.

His comrades await the news of his execution:

DORA: Are we sure that no one will go any further? Sometimes when I listen to Stepan I am afraid. Others perhaps will come who will draw from us authority to kill and who will not pay with their lives.

ANNENKOV: That would be cowardly, Dora.

DORA: Who knows? That perhaps is what justice is, and nobody then will be able to look it in the face.

Stepan brings an eyewitness account of Kaliayev's exection:

DORA (*in a changed, lost voice*): Don't cry. No, no. Don't cry. Can't you see this is the day of justification? . . . Yanek is no longer a murderer. Give me the bomb. (*Annenkov looks at her.*) Yes, next time I want to throw it. I want to be the first to throw it.

ANNENKOV: You know quite well we don't want women in the line of action.

DORA (*crying out*): *Am* I a woman now?
          (*They look at her. Silence.*)

VOINOV (*gently*): Accept, Boria.

STEPAN: Yes. Accept.

ANNENKOV: It was your turn, Stepan.

STEPAN (*looking at Dora*): Accept. She is like me, now.

DORA: You will give it to me, won't you? I'll throw it. And later, on a cold night . . .

ANNENKOV: Yes, Dora?

DORA (*crying*): Yanek, a cold night and the same rope! Everything will be easier now.

CURTAIN

Morally, *L'Homme Révolté* and *Les Justes* are a critique of violence.

Politically, they are a critique of *revolutionary* violence and—most especially—of violence legitimized by the ethos of past revolution. The emphasis falls heavily on the question of the morality of violence used to secure social and political change. The question of violence used to defend the *status quo*—of *force*, in Georges Sorel's terminology—is not considered except in the case where the *status quo* still asserts a legitimacy based on revolution.

Although the concept of revolt is exalted and although several revolutionaries are shown as noble and sympathetic figures, the message of the two works is profoundly antirevolutionary as well as—in a more obvious and superficial sense—anti-Stalinist. Emotionally, the trend of both works is against all violence. Yet Camus never reached, and never really came near, the pacifist position. He does not consider explicitly in what conditions nonrevolutionary violence may be justifiable. When we come to examine his actual political positions of the middle and late 1950s, we shall see the nature and limitations in practice of his critique of the use of violence by Western bourgeois states and specifically by France. In relation to revolutionary violence, his position is sharp and explicit: the only thing that can justify such violence is that he who inflicts it should lay down his life. By the time the revolution comes to power, Stepan alone, out of all the "just men," will survive.

The names of Albert Camus and Jean-Paul Sartre had been associated in the public mind for about ten years. Sartre was already an established figure when *L'Etranger* appeared, and his praise of that novel had helped considerably in bringing the young Camus to the notice of the public. In the immediate post-Liberation period the names of Sartre and Camus had frequently been bracketed together, both as Resistance writers and as existentialists. As early as 1945 Camus had indicated that he thought the bracketing inappropriate, and had denied that he was an existentialist. Unlike Sartre, a teacher of philosophy by profession, Camus can hardly be reckoned a philosopher at all, so that to classify him as belonging to a particular philosophical school makes little sense. In the loose literary and journalistic terminology of the period, however—in which existentialism meant finding life meaningless but finding reasons for carrying on all the same—it was inevitable that Camus's idea of the absurd, as developed in *Le Mythe de Sisyphe* and elsewhere, should be classified as a sort of subvariety of existentialism. Camus was known to have been influenced by Sartre, especially by *La Nausée*, and Sartre's masters—Jaspers, Heidegger, and Kierkegaard—are frequently cited in *Le Mythe de Sisyphe*.

Camus and Sartre met in 1943 and became friends. Politically they worked together fairly closely until 1948. Their positions then began to diverge, in relation to Communism and the Cold War, but it was not until 1951 and 1952, with the publication of *L'Homme Révolté* and of Francis Jeanson's review of it in Sartre's *Les Temps Modernes* that the divergence broke into an open quarrel and the most significant political controversy between intellectuals in the Cold War period.

The nature of the Sartre–Camus quarrel has been seriously distorted, to Sartre's disadvantage, as a result, in part, of the prevailing intellectual climate of the time in the West, in part of a concerted effort, then just beginning, to discredit intellectuals who refused the anti-Communist position, and, in part, of the generally accepted interpretation of the novel *Les Mandarins* by Simone de Beauvoir.

The period was that of Stalin's last years. The Korean war was in progress, and the mood throughout the West was hostile not merely to Stalin, Russia, Communists, and Communism, but also to all persons considered "soft" on Communism. Thus public opinion was—and long remained—predisposed to be for the anti-Communist protagonist in such a controversy.

This tendency, inherent in the nature of the situation, was also deliberately fostered, precisely at the level of the Sartre–Camus controversy, by the efforts, covertly sponsored by the United States government, of a group of intellectuals seeking to accredit the proposition that failure to take an anti-Communist stand constituted "the treason of the clerks" of which Benda spoke. Wherever there was a public capable of interesting itself in the Sartre–Camus controversy, that public was encouraged to see in Camus, not in Sartre, the exemplar of the truly independent intellectual. These efforts continue to be influential in our own day. The account of the controversy best known in America, for example, is that contained in the widely read collection of critical essays edited by Germaine Brée under the title *Camus*. In this collection the essay "Sartre versus Camus, a Political Quarrel"[6] by Nicola Chiaromonte allows no merit whatever to Sartre's side in the controversy and accuses Sartre of being an amateur Communist, intellectually domi-

[6] Originally published in 1952.

nated by the Marxist-Leninist-Stalinist mentality, guilty of moral smugness and intellectual arrogance, and spreading "the intellectual confusion by which the Communist Party benefits." What Mr. Chiaromonte was spreading, on the other hand, was that by which the United States government considered itself to benefit. He was at the time in question director of *Tempo Presente*, the Italian magazine supported by the Congress for Cultural Freedom and—as we now know—then covertly subsidized by the Central Intelligence Agency.[7]

Simone de Beauvoir's novel *Les Mandarins* has generally been treated as a *roman à clef*. It contains a quarrel between Henri and Dubreuilh. Most readers have identified Henri with Camus and Dubreuilh with Sartre. In the novel, the quarrel hinges on whether or not to publish a report revealing the existence and nature of forced-labor camps in the Soviet Union. Both men agree that the reports are true. Dubreuilh nonetheless opposes publishing them because this would serve the interests of the bourgeoisie against the working class. Henri insists on publication.

Simone de Beauvoir, in her autobiography, has denied that *Les Mandarins* is a *roman à clef*. "Henri, whatever people may have said about him, is not

[7] To those who will certainly consider it in bad taste to bring this up, I offer a question: If it could have been established that Sartre's *Les Temps Modernes* stood in the same relation to the government of the Soviet Union as it has been shown that Chiaromonte's *Tempo Presente* stood to that of the United States, would they consider that also irrelevant to a discussion of the controversy?

Camus; not at all. . . . The identification of Sartre with Dubreuilh is not less distorted. . . . The plot which I devised also deliberately departs from the facts."[8]

That Sartre's position on the Soviet labor camps has nothing in common with that of the fictional Dubreuilh is a matter of record: he had published in *Les Temps Modernes* in 1947—long before his break with Camus —a report of the exact nature discussed in *Les Mandarins*.

In fact the quarrel, though significant, was much less dramatic than in *Les Mandarins*. The *amitié distante*—Simone de Beauvoir's term—between Sartre and Camus had for some time been growing less friendly and more distant, and it finally broke down in 1952 with the publication in Sartre's *Les Temps Modernes* of Francis Jeanson's hostile review, with its sarcastic title, "Albert Camus ou l'Âme Révoltée." Camus replied angrily and haughtily in a letter aimed at Sartre personally and affecting to treat Jeanson as merely an instrument of Sartre. Sartre answered Camus in a "come off it" tone and in terms wounding Camus's pride.

Much of the debate was in philosophical language, but its essence was political. In this climate of the Cold War, Sartre and Jeanson continued to adhere to the position which Camus had announced in 1945: the rejection of political anti-Communism and the perception of its "unavowed motives." Sartre had condemned Stalinist crimes (and had in turn been hysteri-

[8] See *La Force des Choses* (Paris, 1963) pp. 288–90.

cally denounced by the Stalinist press in France), but he had refused to treat these crimes as being a logical consequence of Communist doctrine or of revolutionary experience, or to see either Communism or the Soviet bloc as the sole or principal source of evil in the contemporary world. Camus, in "Ni Victimes ni Bourreaux," *L'Homme Révolté,* and *Les Justes,* was asserting the contrary propositions: explicitly in relation to Communism and revolutionary practice, implicitly in relation to the Soviet Union as the main contemporary source of evil.

The general controversy had a practical contemporary and local bearing. France was at this time continuing to wage a full-scale colonial war in Indochina and had also engaged in colonial repression in North Africa and Madagascar. The position of Sartre and his circle was that Frenchmen who hated terror and oppression should turn their attention first to the area of responsibility of their own country. Oppression was detestable, whether of Kirghizes in the Soviet Union or of Malgaches in the French Empire, but for a Frenchman the priority of protest should be: *le Malgache avant le Kirghize.* This question of priority was of the greatest importance, not only politically but psychologically, for Camus, an Algerian Frenchman. It came to press on him more and more insistently in the last decade of his life, and I believe it to be crucial to the assessment of the final phase of his work.

From the very moment of the liberation of France, Camus had foreseen increasing trouble in the colonies, especially in Algeria. He assumed, like almost all Frenchmen—including the Communists, at this time—that France would hold on to its colonial empire, and he even suggested that France would be more conscious of its empire than it had been in the past.

"For those of us who knew colonial policy, the ignorance and indifference of the French about their empire were really frightening. Once again it was a small elite of administrators and great adventurers who gave their compatriots wealth in which they took no interest. Today at least France is too diminished in Europe not to pay attention to all its property. In the balance sheet which we have to draw up it would be unforgivable of us to go on ignoring the lands of the Empire."[9] He points out in the same article that an extension of the franchise among the native population in North Africa will be opposed by the French population. "If the government is to bring to fruition its policy of friendship and protection with [*sic*] the Algerians, it must reason away or reduce this resistance in advance."

> This is of the highest importance, for we must not hide from ourselves that among a manly people like the Arabs defeat entailed a loss of prestige for us. Hence, the French may be tempted, in order to win back a credit lost as a result of force, to display force again. No policy could be blinder. We shall find real support in our colonies only when we shall have convinced them that their interests are ours and that

[9] *Combat*, October 13, 1944. See R. Quilliot (ed.), *Albert Camus: Essais* (Paris, 1965), *Textes Complémentaires* to *Actuelles I*, pp. 1529–31.

we are not applying two separate policies: one giving justice to the people of France and the other legitimizing injustice toward the Empire.

Behind the imperative style of the editorial writer there is an unresolved question. The government must do justice to the Arabs—and it is implied that this justice requires a large extension of the franchise—but before doing so (*auparavant*) it must reason away or reduce (*raisonne ou réduise*) the resistance of the French population to "any policy of enfranchisement of the native people." What happens to the policy of justice for the Arabs if the resistance of the settlers cannot be reasoned away or reduced? In this case one of Camus's "musts" becomes opposed to the other, and his whole thinking on the subject breaks down in self-contradiction. This is in fact what happened.

In May 1945 limited local uprisings occurred in Algeria, mainly in the district of Sétif: "The repression was ruthlessly carried out by the air force and naval artillery. Official death list: 102 European victims; 1500 Moslems—15,000 Moslems according to the Parliamentary Commission of Inquiry."[10] In the wake of these events, Camus visited Algeria and wrote a series of articles for *Combat*.[11] In these he noted that most Arabs no longer wanted French citizenship; he wrote with sympathy but inconclusively about Ferhat Abbas's program for a kind of home rule for Algeria leaving defense and foreign policy in the

[10] Editor's note in Quilliot (ed.), op. cit., p. 1854.
[11] May 1945. Reprinted in *Actuelles III* (*Chroniques Algériennes*).

hands of the Paris government. Camus notes that the mutual ill feeling between French and Arabs in Algeria has been increased by what happened at Sétif and elsewhere. He concludes with an appeal against hatred and in favor of justice: "It is the infinite force of justice, and it alone, which must help us to win back Algeria and its inhabitants." After this there is a silence of nine years. Camus as a journalist or political writer does not again return to the subject of Algeria until 1954, the year in which the revolt began which ended only after Camus's death, with the withdrawal of the French forces from Algeria. During this period the will of the settlers, backed by the metropolitan apparatus of repression, completely prevailed over any ideas of democratization. The elections of 1948 were faked, as Camus and many others acknowledged in 1955. "From the falsified elections," wrote Camus in 1955, "sprang . . . the Algeria of murder and repression."[12] Yet at the time of the elections in question, and until the rebellion, his overt political thinking about revolt and freedom was concentrated on Communism and Russia rather than on his own country. At the same time, at the height of the controversy over *L'Homme Révolté*, Camus denied a charge that he was "not interested in the victims of colonialism" and referred to "hundreds of pages" proving that "for twenty years . . . I have never really conducted any other political struggle except that."[13]

[12] *L'Express*, July 9, 1955. See Quilliot (ed.), op. cit., *Textes Complémentaires* to *Actuelles III*, pp. 1865–72.
[13] *L'Observateur*, June 1952. Quilliot (ed.), op. cit.

In fact Camus had consistently advocated clemency and generosity in dealing with subject peoples of the empire and had advocated a widening of the franchise. The complex of attitudes opposed to these seems to have constituted what he identified as colonialism. This apart, he took the continuance of French rule for granted and he also took for granted that in a country like Algeria the pace of change, in the direction which he desired, would have to be regulated at least to a considerable extent by the feelings of a settler population dominated by the attitudes which he deplored. When rebellion occurrred he deplored it and also deplored the repressions which followed it. When rebellion did not occur he refrained from political comment, although it is probable that in combating Stalinism, for example, he felt himself to be combating the same spiritual forces which he identified as "colonialism."

Yet this was a time when Camus's imagination was coming to grips with Algeria—an Algeria of natives and settlers—more directly than ever before. In the period from 1952 to 1954—that is, on the eve of the outbreak of the Algerian war—Camus wrote six stories which were later collected in the volume *L'Exil et le Royaume*. Four of these stories are set in Algeria, and one of them treats a European-native relationship in another context—that of Brazil.

The first story, "La Femme Adultère," was first published in Algiers in November 1954, the month in which the Algerian war began. It deals with the jour-

ney into the south of Algeria of two Algerian Europeans: Marcel, a shopkeeper in search of textiles, and
his wife, Janine. Their fellow passengers are mostly
Arabs. "Their silence, their impassivity, got on
Janine's nerves. When the bus stopped, the driver rattled
off a few words in that language which she had heard
all her life without ever understanding it." She gets
a start when shepherds gather round the stalled bus.
"On the embankment, quite near the bus, draped
forms stood motionless. Under the hood of the
burnoose, and behind a rampart of veils, only their
eyes could be seen. They were silent. You could not
tell where they had come from; they looked at the
travelers." When they reach the hotel they order coffee,
and an old Arab goes off slowly to get it. " 'Take it
easy in the morning, not too quick in the evening.'
said Marcel, laughing." In the original draft he said
something more, which was eliminated in the published version: " 'And people expect them to develop,'
said Marcel. 'To develop you have to work, and with
them work is like pork, forbidden.' " The editor of
Camus's collected works in the Pléiade edition comments: "One may wonder whether in cutting out these
two sentences [and in other examples which he cites]
Camus was not trying to tone down—taking into account the Algerian war—the spontaneously racist
character of Marcel's reactions."[14]

From the walls of an oasis, Janine looks out at a
nomad camp and envies and desires the nomad life.

[14] R. Quilliot (ed.), *Albert Camus: Théâtre, Récits, Nouvelles*
(Paris, 1965).

In the middle of the night she is conscious of "a dumb call . . . whose meaning she would never understand if she didn't answer it immediately." She rises from her husand's bed and has a kind of mystical communion with the desert night—her "adultery." "After so many years, in which, fleeing before fear, she had run crazily without object, she was stopping at last. At the same time, it seemed to her that she was recovering her roots, the sap was mounting again in her body, which was no longer trembling."

The second story, "Le Renégat," is the interior monologue of a European ex-priest, a prisoner of a desert tribe, which has cut out his tongue. He has become converted to the religion of his masters, and their fetish: "Only evil is present. Down with Europe, reason, honor, and the cross." He has come to hope that "they would mutilate my people as they have mutilated me." The renegade lies in ambush for a missionary and shoots him down. He has a vision of an Arab conquest of Europe: "Oh my masters, they will beat the soldiers, they will beat the word and love. They will cross the deserts and the seas, will fill the light of Europe with their black veils, strike in the belly, yes, strike in the eyes, will sow their salt over the continent. All vegetation, all youth will be extinguished, and dumb crowds with hobbled feet will walk by my side in the desert of the world under the cruel sun of the true faith. I will no longer be alone."

Yet the French army may win. "Wait a little. Where is the city, these noises in the distance and the soldiers perhaps victorious, no, they mustn't be, even if the soldiers are victorious they are not wicked enough. They won't know how to reign. They will say again that you must get better and always again millions of men between evil and good, torn, paralysed, oh, fetish, why has thou abandoned me?"

Dying and delirious, he talks to the wounded missionary. " 'Men who were once my brothers, my only recourse, oh, solitude, don't abandon me! Here, here, who are you, torn and bloody-mouthed, it's you, wizard, the soldiers have conquered you, the salt is burning over there, you are my beloved master! Give up that face of hatred, be kind now, we were mistaken, we will begin again, we will rebuild the city of mercy, I want to go home. Yes, help me. That's right. Give me your hand. Give . . .' A handful of salt filled the mouth of the chatterbox slave."

"La Femme Adultère" and "Le Renégat" are a diptych of heaven and hell, like Mauriac's "Le Mystère Frontenac" and "Le Rang." Just as Mauriac's feelings about his mother turned to idyll in one story and nightmare in the other, so do Camus's feelings about Algeria.

The third story, "Les Muets," is about a labor dispute in a cooper's shop in the Algeria of Camus's youth. The men have to go back to work after a strike. They have been on friendly terms with their employer but now hold him at arm's length. The employer's small daughter falls suddenly ill and is taken away in an ambulance. The men would like to express their sympathy but are too awkward and tongue-tied to do so. In the evening one of the workers tells his wife what has happened. The story ends with the words: "When he had finished, he sat motionless, looking toward the sea, where the quick twilight ran from one end to the other of the horizon. 'Oh, it's his fault!' said he. He would have liked to be young and for Fernande to be young too and they would have gone away to the other side of the sea."

The fourth story, "L'Hôte," is Camus's most direct approach, in his imaginative writing, to the political situation in Algeria. It is about Daru, a schoolteacher in the *bled*, to whom a European policeman brings an Arab prisoner. The policeman is on horseback. He leads the Arab, who is on foot, by a rope. The poor, hard life of Daru as a teacher is described: "The country was like that, cruel to live in, even without the men, who, however, didn't make things any easier. But Daru was born there. Anywhere else he felt himself in exile."

The policeman asks Daru to take the Arab to the nearest town. Daru is reluctant. The policeman, Balducci, says, "The orders are there and they affect you too. There's trouble starting, it seems. Talk of a revolt in the near future. We are mobilized in a way."[15]

The policeman explains that the Arab is charged

[15] "Was 'L'Hôte' conceived under the Algerian crisis? If by that is meant the drama which burst out in all its violence on All Saints' Day, 1954, certainly not. . . . Yet from [1952] on, the political evolution of Algeria so preoccupied Camus that the draft of his story bears the mark of anxiety. He was fully aware of the revolt which was brewing." (Quilliot (ed.), *Camus: Théâtre,* . . . p. 2040.)

with the murder of his cousin. The teacher asks, "He is against us?" The policeman replies, "I don't know. You can never tell."

In the original manuscript this was sharper: " 'Oh? He's not a rebel?' 'They all are, my boy. But this one is a common-law criminal.' "

The policeman leaves the Arab with the teacher, who "cursed both his own people, who had sent him this Arab, and the Arab, who had dared to kill and who had not been capable of getting away." Daru does not take the Arab to prison but gives him provisions for the journey and watches him "walk off slowly on the road to prison."

Returning to his school, Daru finds written on the blackboard in clumsy characters the inscription: YOU BETRAYED OUR BROTHER. YOU WILL PAY. And the story ends with the words: "Daru looked at the sky, the plateau and beyond the invisible lands which stretched down to the sea. In this vast country which he had loved so much, he was alone."

The original manuscript stopped with the Arab walking to prison; there was no reference to threats.

The second version ends: "YOU BETRAYED MY BROTHER. YOUR SCHOOL WILL BURN AND YOU WITH IT. Daru looked unseeing at the light springing from the heights of the sky all over the surface of the plateau. In this vast country, which had been his, he was alone."

In the third version, there are three variants in Camus's hand: "In this vast country without which he could not live—with which he made one—which remained his only native land."

Roger Quilliot remarks that "the pluperfect finally chosen—'which he had loved so much'—is like a renunciation and a farewell."[16]

The fifth story, "Jonas," the only one in a metropolitan setting, is about a successful artist who ceases to be able to paint. The tone is one of painful, grating irony, reflecting Camus's bitterness and sense of isolation at the time of the quarrel with Sartre and his circle. Jonas becomes a kind of prisoner of his family and his friends. He subscribes to good causes, gives advice, even signs protests, against the advice of his only real friend, Rateau: "You're going in for politics now? Leave that to writers and ugly girls."

Jonas takes to drink and women, ceases to paint. Then one day he brings home planks and builds for himself a kind of shed under the ceiling of his high apartment room. To this he retires, announcing that he has to paint. He stays there in the dark for a long time. Then he lights a lamp and calls for a canvas. He works all night; in the morning he is happy and collapses. He will recover. The story ends with his friend, Rateau, looking at "the canvas, entirely blank, in the center of which Jonas had written only, in very small characters, a word which you could make out, but without knowing whether it should be read as *solitaire* or *solidaire*."

The last story, "La Pierre qui Pousse" ("The Growing Stone"), is set in Brazil. The central figure is D'Arrast, a visting French engineer. D'Arrast makes the acquaintance of a black ship's cook, with whom he

[16] Ibid., p. 2044.

attends a voodoo ceremony. The cook, in danger of death at sea, made a vow to Jesus that he would carry, on a feast-day procession in his native town, "a stone of fifty kilos on his head." The cook asks D'Arrast whether he had ever "called" or made a promise. D'Arrast hesitates and then says yes.

"Someone was going to die. It was my fault. I think I called."
"Did you promise?"
"No, I would have liked to promise."

D'Arrast watches the procession and the cook, "visibly exhausted . . . bent under the huge stone."

D'Arrast helps the cook on his way, but the stone slips from the cook's head and he collapses. D'Arrast takes the stone on his own head and walks on with it. Instead of taking it to the church, however—as vowed by the cook—he takes it to the cook's hut and there throws it down on the fire in the middle of the room. "There . . . drinking in with desperate gulps the smell of poverty and ashes which he recognized, he listened to a wave rising in him of a dark and panting joy to which he could not give a name."

The cook's family, led by his brother, gathers round. D'Arrast stands in the dark "with his eyes shut. He joyously saluted his own strength. He saluted once again life beginning again. . . . The brother moved away a little from the cook and half turning toward D'Arrast, without looking at him, showed him the empty place: 'Sit down with us.' "

D'Arrast's experience is in some ways similar to Janine's. In both cases there is a sort of mystical orgasm of communion with a remote people, rather like the Miltonic total interpenetration of angels. Both scenes have a dreamlike quality, as also has the horror of "Le Renégat" and Jonas's shed. The "kingdom" in these stories is one of fantasy. The exile is real, and from it stems the fantasy of the kingdom. The variant endings of "L'Hôte" are our most direct evidence of how much that exile meant to Camus.

Camus's political writings on the Algerian war are collected in *Actuelles III* (*Chroniques Algériennes*), which he published in 1958. It is a depressing volume. The manner, in the post-1945 essays, is not so much that of Camus as that of the moderate bourgeois French journalism of the period: categorical and resonant in tone, equivocal in substance. "The Arab personality will be recognized by the French personality, but in order for that to happen, France must exist. 'You must choose your side,' cry the haters. Oh, I have chosen it! I have chosen my country. I have chosen the Algeria of justice in which French and Arabs will associate freely!" He had one concrete idea during this early part of the war—that of a "truce for civilians." He went to Algeria in January 1956 and presented this idea at a public meeting. The proposal was badly received. Camus was barracked by the Europeans, largely ignored by the Moslems. An informant of Albert Memmi spoke of his disappointment at Camus's "sweet sister" speech.

The dual crisis of the autumn of 1956—Suez and Hungary—brought a closer assimilation of Camus's position to that of the French right-of-center. He supported the Hungarian rebels—as did Sartre—but, unlike Sartre, drew "European" lessons from their action: "In spite of the dramatic bankruptcy of the traditional movements and ideals of the Left, the real Europe exists united in justice and in liberty, confronting all tyrannies."[17] In relation to Suez, the only violence which he condemned was that of the language of Marshal Bulganin.[18] In a message to French students on Hungary he acclaimed "that violent and pure force which drives men and peoples to claim the honor of living upright."[19] At the same time, he believed that as a result of the lesson of Hungary "we will be less tempted to overwhelm our own nation, and it alone, under the weight of its historic sins. We will be more careful—without ceasing to demand from her all the justice of which she is capable—about her survival and her liberty."[20] The France whose survival was in question was a France which included Algeria: thus the rightness of the Hungarian rebellion provided a reason for putting down the Algerian one. In respect of methods, his position remained humane: torture was "as contemptible in Algiers as in Budapest."[21] Hope nonetheless resided exclusively in the Western

[17] *Franc-Tireur*, November 10, 1956. Quilliot (ed.), *Camus: Essais*, p. 1780.
[18] *Tempo Presente/Demain*, February 1957. Quilliot (ed.), *Camus: Essais*, p. 1763.
[19] Message to a meeting of French students, November 23, 1956. Quilliot (ed.), *Albert Camus: Essais*, p. 1781.
[20] Ibid.
[21] Discours de la Salle Wagram, March 5, 1957. Quilliot (ed.), *Camus: Essais*, p. 1783.

camp. "The defects of the West are numberless, its crimes and its faults real. But in the last analysis, let us not forget that we are the only people who hold that power of improvement and emancipation which reside in the genius of freedom (*le libre génie*)."[22]

Despite his revulsion from the methods of the repression, his position was necessarily one of support for repression, since he consistently opposed negotiation with the actual leaders of the rebellion, the FLN. In 1955 he had proposed an Algerian round table without the FLN, and in 1958, in the foreword to his *Chroniques Algériennes (Actuelles III)*, he points out that negotiation with the FLN would lead to "the independence of Algeria controlled by the most implacable military leaders of the insurrection; that is to say, the eviction of 1,200,000 Europeans of Algeria and the humiliation of millions of Frenchmen, with the risks involved in that humiliation." He makes it clear that he rejects this independence, and therefore the negotiation. The rejection of negotiation is basic and necessarily implies support for the substance, if not for the details of the methods, of the French government's policy of pacification. The actual political formulas proposed by Camus in 1958 have to be situated in the light of this: they are formulas of a type frequently canvassed and varied by French governments at this period, designed to help the process of pacification—through the isolation of the FLN—and capable of execution only after the suppression of the FLN, if at all. Thus the regime of "free associa-

22 Ibid.

tion" which he foresaw required French military victory over the insurgents. After that he aspired to the extension of democratic rights to the Arab population, but the results of this democratic process could be overruled from France. The French government was urged to announce: "One: that it is disposed to give full justice to the Arab people of Algeria and to liberate it from the colonial system; two: that it will make no concession on the question of the rights of the French of Algeria; three: that it cannot accept that the justice which it will consent to render should signify for the French nation the prelude for a sort of historic death and for the West the risk of an encirclement which would lead to the kadarization of Europe and the isolation of America."[23]

Camus's position in the 1950s was one of extreme intellectual and emotional difficulty and tension. He had written about freedom, justice, violence, and revolt in abstract terms, and asserted principles which he presented as of both fundamental importance and universal application. He never altogether abandoned this language, and he continued to write about politics in the tone of a severe moralist. Yet his actual positions were political and partisan. The violence of the Hungarian rebels and of the Anglo-French expedition in Egypt raised no problems. It was violence "on the right side"—precisely the logic he had rejected, on grounds of a rigorous morality, in relation to revolutionary violence. Freedom was an absolute for the Hungarians, and their violence in asserting their will

[23] *Algérie 1958* in *Chroniques Algériennes* (*Actuelles III*).

"to stand upright" was "pure." The violence of the
Algerian Arabs, who thought that they were making the
same claim, was "inexcusable," and the nature and
degree of the freedom to be accorded to them were
matters to be decided by France, in the light of its own
strategic needs—a plea which was irrelevant when
made by Russia.

He remained in fact a Frenchman of Algeria, and
what seemed to be the increasingly right-wing positions of his later years were latent in his earlier silences. The only public statement of Camus on the
subject of the Algerian war that has the ring of com-
plete candor is one that he made in Sweden in December 1957, just after he had received the Nobel Prize:
"I have always condemned terror. I must also condemn
a terrorism which operates blindly, in the streets of
Algiers for example, and which one day may strike my
mother or my family. I believe in justice, but I will
defend my mother before justice."[24]

The defense of his mother required support for the
French army's pacification of Algeria.

It is only in the light of this situation, with all its
conflicts and ironies, that one can understand Camus's
last and perhaps his best novel, *La Chute* (*The Fall*).

La Chute began as a story for *L'Exil et le Royaume*
and is marked by some of the same preoccupations as
the stories in that collection. The place of exile is
Holland, the setting a dockside bar. The story is cast

[24] Stockholm interview, December 14, 1957. Quilliot (ed.),
Camus: Essais, pp. 1881–82.

in the form of a monologue; the narrator is Jean-Baptiste Clamence, once a lawyer, now describing himself as "a penitent judge" (*juge pénitent*).[25] Clamence's style is elaborate and ceremonious: "I see you gag at that imperfect subjunctive. I must confess my weakness for that form and for fine language in general." One of the reproaches that had stung Camus most at the time of the publication of *L'Homme Révolté* was that of excessive elegance in style; in the person of Clamence he gives this tendency full rein, while partly parodying it, and taunts his adversaries. He diagnoses that his interlocutor is a bourgeois, but a "refined bourgeois! To gag over imperfect subjunctives indeed proves your culture twice over, since you recognize them in the first place and then since they irritate you."

The setting, like so much in *L'Exil et le Royaume*, is dreamlike. "Holland is a dream, sir. A dream of gold and smoke. More smoky by day and more gold by night. Did you notice that the concentric canals of Amsterdam are like the circles of hell? A bourgeois hell, naturally, peopled with bad dreams."

Clamence tells of his life in Paris as a lawyer: "I specialized in noble causes. . . . I had my heart on my sleeve. You would have really thought that justice slept with me every night." He abounded in small courtesies, was generous, lived a full life. "I succeeded in loving at the same time women and justice, which is

[25] This is probably a reference to the penitent orders of friars, who both do penance themselves and suggest penance to others.

not easy. I went in for sports and fine arts. . . . I was made to have a body, hence that harmony in me, that easy mastery which people felt and which helped them to live, they sometimes told me. In truth, through being a man, with so much plenitude and simplicity, I became a little bit of a superman."

One day when coming back from court after making "a brilliant improvisation . . . on the hardness of heart of our ruling class," Clamence was crossing the Pont des Arts when he heard a laugh behind him, looked round, and saw no one there: "The laugh had nothing mysterious about it. It was a good laugh, friendly." That evening when Clamence saw his face in the bathroom mirror "it seemed to me that my smile was double."

He tells of another incident which altered his picture of himself. Getting out of his car to remonstrate with a stalled motorcyclist who refuses to move and uses abusive language, he is hit in the face by a pedestrian who takes the side of the motorcyclist. Behind his car, a line of traffic starts to honk horns. He returns to his car and drives off while the pedestrian taunts him with cowardice. "After having been struck in public without reacting, it was no longer possible for me to caress that beautiful image of myself." He dreams of revenge. "The truth is that every intelligent man dreams of being a gangster and of ruling over society through violence alone. As that is not as easy as you might think by reading certain kinds of novels, one generally relies on politics and runs to the cruelest party. What does it matter, after all, to humiliate one's mind if in that way you can succeed in dominating everybody? I discovered in myself sweet dreams of oppression."

He tells of a kind of love affair. He learns that a woman with whom he once slept has told a third party that he was not much good. He takes care to recapture this woman, dominate her, and mortify her. "Until the day when in the violent disorder of a painful and constrained pleasure, she rendered homage aloud to what enslaved her. On that day I started to get farther away from her since I had forgotten her."

The he tells of his "essential discovery": Crossing the Pont Royal in Paris one night in November, three years before the evening when he heard the laugh, he sees a young woman leaning over the parapet. After passing her, he hears the noise of a body falling into the water. He stops without turning round. He hears a cry repeated several times, going down the river and then ceasing. He listens for a while, then walks off with short steps in the rain. "I informed nobody."

His relations with his friends change. "My fellows ceased to be in my eyes the respectful audience I was used to. The circle of which I was the center broke, and they placed themselves in a single row, as on a courthouse bench. . . . Yes, they were there as before but they were laughing. . . . The whole universe started laughing around me."

Clamence is pursued by a ridiculous thought: "One could not die without having confessed all one's lies. Not to God or one of his representatives. I was above that, as you may imagine. No—to confess it to men, to a friend or a woman one loved, for example." He cherishes such projects as jostling blind men in the street, bursting the tires of wheelchairs, and slapping infants in the subway. "The very word 'justice' threw me into strange furies."

One day on a transatlantic liner he sees a black spot on the ocean. He looks away, his heart beating. When he looks back, the black spot has disappeared. It bobs up again, a piece of flotsam. "Yet I had not been able to look at it. I had thought immediately of a drowned person. I understood then, with acceptance, as one resigns oneself to an idea whose truth one has known for a long time, that that cry which years before had rung out on the Seine behind me had not ceased, carried by the river towards the waters of the Channel, to make its way in the world across the vast space of the ocean and that it had waited for me until this day when I met it again. I understood also that it would continue to wait for me on the seas and on the rivers—everywhere where might be found the bitter water of my baptism. Even here, tell me, are we not on the water?"

He speaks of the guilt of Jesus for the deaths of the Innocents. "That sadness which you can make out in all his acts. Was it not the incurable melancholy of one who heard throughout the nights the voice of Rachel, groaning over her little ones and refusing all consolation? The cry rose in the night. Rachel called her children, killed for him, and he was living."

He realizes that he is again pleading a case. He is half advocate, half prophet: "After all, that's what I am, taking asylum in a wilderness of stone, of fog and stagnant water. An empty prophet for a mediocre time. Elijah without a Messiah. Crammed with fever and alcohol, my back stuck to this mildewed door, my finger lifted toward a lowering sky, covering with curses lawless men who cannot bear any judgment."

He takes to his bed, suffering from "swamp fever, I think, which I picked up when I was Pope." This was during the war, in North Africa, when Clamence had been neutral between the opposing parties and subsequently interned by the Germans. A fellow prisoner proposes that they should choose from among themselves a new Pope who would live among the suffering people. " 'Who among us,' he said, 'has the most weaknesses?' By way of a joke I raised my finger, and was the only one who did. 'Good. Jean-Baptiste will do.' " He exercises his pontificate for a few weeks, his main problem being the distribution of water in the camp. He gives up after drinking the water of a dying comrade. "Persuading myself that the others needed me more than they did the man who was going to die anyway, and that I should keep myself alive for them. This is the way, my friend, that empires and churches are born, under the sun of death."

He explains how he carried on his new profession of penitent judge, by the practice of public confession. "I mix together what concerns me and what has to do with other people. I take common characteristics, experiences which we have suffered together, weaknesses which we share, good manners, present-day man, in short, as he rages in me and in others. With all that, I make a portrait which is one of everybody and nobody. A mask, in short, quite like a carnival—one recognizable and simplified, one in front of which you say: 'I think I've met that fellow somewhere!' When the portrait is finished, as this evening, I show it with an air of grief: 'That, alas, is what I am.' The indictment is finished. But at the same moment the portrait which I show to my contemporaries becomes a mirror."

He confesses that he is in possession of the stolen panel, "The Just Judges," from van Eyck's *The Mystic Lamb*. He thinks his interlocutor may be a policeman and invites him to make an arrest. This interlocutor is, however, like himself, a lawyer; they are "of the same race." Clamence addresses to him the last words of *La Chute*: "Tell me, I beg you, what happened to you one evening on the banks of the Seine and how you succeeded in never risking your life. Say to yourself the words which for years have not ceased to ring out during my nights and which I will say at last through your mouth: 'Young girl, throw yourself in the water again, so that I can have a second chance to save us both.' A second chance, eh? What a rash suggestion! Supposing, sir, we were to be taken at our word, we'd have to carry out our promise. Brrrrrr! The water is so cold! But don't worry. It's too late now. It will always be too late—luckily!"

Roger Quilliot rightly warns that to try "to identify Camus with Clamence would be as gross an error as to insist on mixing him up with Tarrou."

Emmett Parker says that "Jean-Baptiste Clamence, rather than being a modern John the Baptist, Clamens [*sic*] in Deserto, as many critics have thought, comes near to being a satirical portrait of left-wing intellectuals as Camus saw them, lost in the nihilistic desert of twentieth-century ideologies, led astray by their own systematic abstractions."[26]

Even though the novel contains, as M. Quilliot has established, many echoes of the Sartre–Camus controversy and not a few gibes at the Sartre position, it would be a serious error, and a belittling one, to take Clamence as a kind of caricature of "Sartre and other progressive intellectuals." Clamence himself surely gives the clue when he says, "I mix together what concerns me and what has to do with others." It is a "game of mirrors," as Camus himself said. It is inconceivable that Camus, the Saint-Just of 1944, "the godless saint" of post-Liberation youth, could have devised the character of the penitent judge without his irony being aimed at himself as well as at others. The book is not "satirical" in any ordinary sense; its irony is wry and painful, its tone that of the *examen de conscience* which stands in the background of the French moralistic tradition to which Camus consciously belonged. *La Chute* is not a caricature but a probing of man's nature as known to Camus through his own experience: Clamence is certainly not Camus, but is the arrangement of mirrors through which Camus inspects that experience and causes it to be

[26] Emmett Parker, *Albert Camus: the Artist in the Arena* (Madison and Milwaukee, 1955), p. 160.

reflected. Nor can the specifically Christian or pre-Christian elements in *La Chute*—so clearly signaled both in the title and in the name of the narrator-protagonist—be glossed over. Under its surface of irony and occasional blasphemy, *La Chute* is profoundly Christian in its confessional form, in its imagery, and above all in its pervasive message that it is only through the full recognition of our sinful nature that we can hope for grace. Grace does not, it is true, arrive, and the novel ends on what is apparently a pessimistic note. Yet the name of the narrator—that of the forerunner—hints, however teasingly, at the possibility of a sequel.[27]

La Chute belongs to the same cycle as the stories in *L'Exil et le Royaume*, although it was not finished until later. Its preoccupations should, I think, be related to those of the stories in that collection, to Camus's sense of isolation after the publication of *L'Homme Révolté*, and especially to his sense of exile resulting from the developing tragedy in his own country. The isolation and the exile are of course connected, because it was Camus's position in relation to Algeria, and therefore to other colonial situations, which marked him off from the political positions of the Sartre circle, reversing their order of priorities between *Kirghize* and *Malgache*.

[27] When in a review in *The Spectator* of the English version of *La Chute* I stressed its Christian tendency, Camus wrote to his English publishers, Hamish Hamilton, confirming that this approach to the novel was sound.

I believe that *La Chute*, the only one of Camus's novels which is not set in Algeria, is the one in which Algeria is most painfully present. Amsterdam is not only an anti-Algeria, a sunless, foggy place of exile; it is also a limbo. "You know, then, that Dante accepts the existence of angels who were neutral in the quarrel between God and Satan. And he puts them in limbo, a sort of antechamber of his hell. We are in the antechamber, my friend."

It is not, I think, fanciful to relate this concept of limbo to Camus's position on the struggle in his native Algeria. Torn between justice and his mother, Camus was drawn into a long hesitation which seemed to many like neutrality. Eventually, with the decision to put his mother first, he came by 1958 to support everything that was fundamental in the French government's position (see page 90). At the time of the writing of *La Chute*, and even later, his position seemed indecisive and unsatisfactory to both communities in Algeria. Naturally the community that resented this most was his own: that of the Europeans, who showed him clearly what they thought in January 1956 (see page 88).

This seems to me to cast some light on the call and the laugh in *La Chute*. Daru in "L'Hôte" was doubly summoned: the policeman, Balducci, called on him to convey the prisoner to the nearest town. The prisoner called him to help the rebels: "*Viens avec nous.*" Daru does not follow either call and is left in isolation—essentially Camus's position. I believe that in *La Chute*

—a much more complex work than "L'Hôte"—these two calls were pressing on Camus's consciousness at this time and fused at a deep level into one: the voice of Rachel calling her children. Clamence's paralysis on the bridge corresponds to that of his creator, before the conflicting call of what he had thought of as his country. The laughter which follows him, which "put things in their proper places," is provoked by the discrepancy between what he has been saying and how he behaves. He who talked so much of justice must now abjure such language, since there is something he prefers to justice. The emergence of the ironical *juge pénitent* prepared the way for a different view of life, more conservative and more organic. Essentially Camus is beginning to take the side of his own tribe against the abstract entities. He is heeding that call which reached him most deeply, thus taking an ironic distance from those universals which had hitherto dominated his language. Perhaps for this reason there is a curious sense of liberation about *La Chute* as compared with the stories in *L'Exil et le Royaume*. The manner of the short stories is generally flat and grating, suggestive of painful effort. In *La Chute*, on the other hand, beneath the bitter irony, there is a return of that undertone of elation which we find in *L'Etranger* and *La Peste*. It is doubtful whether lyricism and irony were ever before so combined as they are in Clamence's narrative. The circles of hell are also a sort of circus, with Clamence as the master showman, virtuoso in the manipulation of mirrors and in a patter which constantly amalgamates the ridiculous and the sublime.

On February 13, 1960, Albert Camus was killed in a motor accident at a place called Villeblerin. He was forty-seven.

La Chute, which implied a renewal, remained his last word.

Probably no European writer of his time left so deep a mark on the imagination and, at the same time, on the moral and political consciousness of his own generation and of the next. He was intensely European because he belonged to the frontier of Europe and was aware of a threat. The threat also beckoned to him. He refused, but not without a struggle.

No other writer, not even Conrad, is more representative of the Western consciousness and conscience in relation to the non-Western world. The inner drama of his work is the development of this relation, under increasing pressure and in increasing anguish.

Many articles and commentators identified Camus as the just man. In this they were unjust to him, perhaps even more so than Madame de Beauvoir when she wrote of him as "that just man without justice" (*ce juste sans justice*). Both verdicts shrink the dimensions of the tragedy. He was above all an artist, and his primary and most enduring concern was not with justice but with artistic truth. Yet the artistic truth of the novelist, dramatist, and essayist has social and political implications and is a form of justice.

In *L'Etranger*, artistic truth was contrasted with, and placed above, forms of justice in society. In *La Peste*, artistic truth joins, through a basic human integrity, an ideal of social and political justice. But *La Chute* breaks up that marriage; artistic truth here reveals justice as a complex and self-flattering illusion.

In historical terms, the ideal of revolutionary justice which was appropriate to a Frenchman under the Occupation (*La Peste*) was no longer appropriate to a Frenchman involved in France's position in the postwar world, and especially not to a Frenchman of Algeria (*La Chute*). Both artistic truth and justice had their social and cultural habitat. Camus was a creation of French history, French culture, and French education, and all the more intensely French because of the insecurity of the frontier. He liked to express himself in universal terms; that too was a French tradition. He could not divest himself of his Frenchness; he could not betray his mother; if France in Algeria was unjust, then it was justice that had to go, yielding place to irony. Rieux and Tarrou made way for Jean-Baptiste Clamence.

Camus's basic dilemma is that of all intellectuals in the advanced countries, in their relation to the poor countries, but with the difference that he felt the dilemma much more acutely and faced the implications of the choice he made, in *La Chute*, with unmatched imaginative integrity. Not every intellectual has to make the same final choice, but each must realize how much he is a product of the culture of the advanced world, and how much there is which will pull him, among the "Algerias" of the future, toward Camus's "fall." One may still feel it to be a fall indeed, a great personal tragedy, and a defeat for a

generation: a defeat most decisive when unacknowl-
edged. One may feel—as the present writer does—that
Sartre and Jeanson were right, and that Camus's voice,
added to theirs instead of turned against them, would
have rallied opinion more decisively and earlier
against imperialist wars, not only in Algeria but also
in Indochina–Vietnam and elsewhere. One may experience horror at the sight of the moral capital of *La
Peste* being drawn on in support of the values of the
Cold War and colonial war. Yet we must recognize
that it was to Camus, not to Sartre, that the choice was
presented in a personal and agonizing form, that
Sartre's choice, even if it was the right one, came
relatively easily,[28] whereas Camus's choice, wrong as
we may think it politically, issued out of the depths
of his whole life-history. Politically, Camus and his
tribe, the Europeans of Algeria, were casualties of the
postwar period. Imaginatively, Camus both flinched
from the realities of his position as a Frenchman of
Algeria, and also explored with increasing subtlety
and honesty the nature and consequences of his flinch-
ing. The moralist talks himself out of existence in the
terrible hollow, public rhetoric of these last years.
At a different, much quieter level, the serious explora-
tions of the mature artist have hardly begun when they
are suddenly cut short by senseless accidental death.

Among those who mourned him, in all the world's
great cities and some other places, there were many
who still thought of him as the just man, the godless

[28] "Relatively" must be stressed. Sartre's choice may have
been easy subjectively, but it involved the risk of his life.

saint. Others, who could no longer think of him in this way, mourned mainly for the artist and for what might still have been. The paradox and torment of his political development presented themselves to us no longer in terms of conscious choices, but as the conditions of the life of the artist—conditions in which *La Chute* represented a heroic achievement. He left us at last the tone, the smile, and the half-promise of Jean-Baptiste Clamence; and also the mirror.

SHORT BIBLIOGRAPHY
INDEX

SHORT BIBLIOGRAPHY

The general edition of Camus's works used in the present study is the *Œuvres Complètes*. Paris: Bibliothèque de la Pléiade (Gallimard):

I. *Théâtre, Récits, Nouvelles*. Roger Quilliot, ed. 1965.

II. *Essais*. Roger Quilliot, ed. 1965.

Editions of the novels and short stories of Camus are as follows:

L'Etranger. Paris, 1942. *The Stranger*. Stuart Gilbert, translator. New York: Knopf, 1946; Vintage Books, 1954.

La Peste. Paris, 1947. *The Plague*. Stuart Gilbert, translator. New York: Knopf, 1948.

La Chute. Paris, 1956. *The Fall*. Justin O'Brien, translator. New York: Knopf, 1957.

L'Exil et le Royaume. Paris, 1957. *Exile and the Kingdom*. Justin O'Brien, translator. New York: Knopf, 1958.

Editions of essays by Camus are:

Le Mythe de Sisyphe. Paris, 1942.

Noces. Paris, 1947.

L'Envers et L'Endroit. Paris, 1958.

The Myth of Sisyphus and Other Essays. Justin O'Brien, translator. New York: Vintage Books, 1960.

Actuelles I (Chroniques 1944–1948). Paris, 1950.

Actuelles II (1948–1953). Paris, 1953.

Actuelles II (Chroniques 1948–1953). Paris, 1953.

Actuelles III (Chroniques Algériennes 1939–1958). Paris, 1958.

Resistance, Rebellion and Death. Justin O'Brien, translator. New York: Knopf, 1961.

L'Homme Révolté. Paris, 1951.

The Rebel. Anthony Bower, translator. New York: Knopf, 1954; Vintage Books, 1956.

Lyrical and Critical Essays. Philip Thody, ed. Ellen Conroy Kennedy, translator. New York: Knopf, 1968. A useful edition of Camus's essays, containing some of the material listed above.

Camus's *Notebooks* (*Carnets*, Volumes I and II) are now in two volumes in English:

The Notebooks: Volume I, 1935–1942. Philip Thody, translator. New York: Knopf, 1963.

The Notebooks: Volume II, 1942–1951. Justin O'Brien, translator. New York: Knopf, 1966.

Some book-length studies of Camus are:

Brée, Germaine. *Camus.* New Brunswick, N.J.: Rutgers University Press, 1961; revised, New York: Harcourt, Brace, Harbinger Edition, 1964.

Brisville, Jean-Claude. *Camus.* Paris, 1959.

Cruickshank, John. *Albert Camus and the Literature of Revolt.* New York: Galaxy, 1960.

de Luppé, Roger. *Albert Camus.* Paris, 1958.

Quilliot, Roger. *La Mer et les Prisons: Essai sur Albert Camus.* Paris, 1956. Contains an extensive bibliography of works by Camus.

Thody, Philip. *Albert Camus: A Study of His Work.* New York: Macmillan, 1957; Evergreen, 1959.

Michel-Antoine Burnier, *Choice of Action*, New York: Random House, 1968, contains a perceptive essay by Bernard Murchland on the "Sartre-Camus controversy." Emmett Parker, *Albert Camus: The Artist in the Arena*, Madison and Milwaukee: University of Wisconsin Press, 1965, presents a conventionally idealized Camus but contains some useful documentation. Anne Durand, *Le Cas Albert Camus*, Paris, 1961, is spiteful and somewhat incoherent, but sheds some interesting light on Camus's early life in Algeria.

Biographical data on Camus are rather scanty. The fullest sources known to me are Quilliot's notes in the Pléiade Edition.

INDEX